ESSAYS
LITERARY & EDUCATIONAL

E. M. W. TILLYARD
LITT.D., F.B.I.

GREENWOOD PRESS, PUBLISHERS
WESTPORT, CONNECTICUT

Library of Congress Cataloging in Publication Data

Tillyard, Eustace Mandeville Wetenhall, 1889-1962.
    Essays, literary & educational.

    Reprint of the ed. published by Chatto & Windus,
London.
    Includes index.
    1. English literature--History and criticism--
Addresses, essays, lectures. I. Title.
[PR99.T56 1978]   820'.9   78-2020
ISBN 0-313-20359-8

820.9
T579es

Reprinted with the permission of Chatto & Windus Ltd.

Reprinted in 1978 by Greenwood Press, Inc.
51 Riverside Avenue, Westport, CT. 06880

Printed in the United States of America

10 9 8 7 6 5 4 3 2 1

CONTENTS

Preface   *page* 7

Acknowledgements   9

I. LITERARY

The Nature of Comedy and Shakespeare (1958)   13

The Trial Scene in *The Merchant of Venice* (1960)   30

Shakespeare's Historical Cycle: Organism or Compilation? (1953)   39

Why did Shakespeare write *Henry VIII*? (1960)   47

Reality and Fantasy in Elizabethan Literature (1956)   55

The Literary Kinds and Milton (1957)   71

A Note on Dryden's Criticism (1950)   80

William Collins's *Ode on the Death of Thomson* (1956)   89

Scott's Linguistic Vagaries (1957)   99

Shelley's *Ozymandias* (1956)   108

Thomas Love Peacock (1955)   114

The Origins of English Anti-Romanticism (1951)   130

Conrad's *Secret Agent* Reconsidered (1960)   144

Is a new History of Criticism possible? (1948)   154

A Mirror for Magistrates Revisited (1958)   165

II. EDUCATIONAL

Two ways of Learning (1954)   185

Research in the Humanities (1947)   192

Lilies or Dandelions? (1955)   204

On Annotating *Paradise Lost* IX and X for Schools (1960)   209

Index   219

ERRATA

On title page, *F.B.I.* should be *F.B.A.*
On page 119, line 12, the word *sitting* should be *siting*.

PREFACE

The essays that compose this book are miscellaneous; and I must ask the reader to remember that they were not all addressed to the same kind of audience. *Reality and Fantasy in Elizabethan Literature* and *Thomas Love Peacock* are more popular than the rest, assuming little knowledge of their themes. At the other end of the scale, *Shakespeare's Historical Cycle* takes for granted a fresh knowledge of the plays concerned and had better be avoided by those who lack it. The rest lie somewhere between these two extremes.

Research in the Humanities embodies a lecture given at various Canadian universities under the auspices of the Humanities Research Council of Canada and should be read as so doing.

Although I wrote up the *Origins of English Anti-Romanticism* in 1951 I based it on notes for a lecture within a course for the English Tripos at Cambridge in the early thirties, when the reaction against the Romantics was at its height; and I fancy that in tone it belongs to the earlier date.

The literary essays are printed according to the dates of their subjects except *"A Mirror for Magistrates" Revisited*, which comes last instead of first. I made the exception so that this essay could come next to the first of the educational essays, which also has things to say about the *Mirror*.

A few sentences in *The Literary Kinds and Milton* and in *Conrad's "Secret Agent" Reconsidered* are repeated from the *Nature of Comedy and Shakespeare*. There seemed little point in saying the same things (which needed saying) in other words; and I hope the reader will not be irritated by the repetition.

The date added to the title of each essay in the table of contents is that of composition. Most of the essays have been published before; and I have given details of the place and date of publication on the Acknowledgements page.

E. M. W. T.

ACKNOWLEDGEMENTS

"The Nature of Comedy and Shakespeare" was the Presidential Address to the English Association for 1958. "The Trial Scene in *The Merchant of Venice*" was published in *A Review of English Literature*, October 1961; "Shakespeare's Historical Cycle" in *Studies in Philology*, January 1954; "Why did Shakespeare write *Henry VIII?*" in *Critical Quarterly*, Spring 1961. "Reality and Fantasy in Elizabethan Literature" was a lecture given at the Comburg Academy, Würtemberg, and published in *Lehrgangsvortraege der Akademie Comburg*, 1956. "The Literary Kinds and Milton" was a lecture given at the triennial conference of the Fédération Internationale des Langues Modernes held at Heidelberg in 1957. "A Note on Dryden's Criticism" is reprinted from *The Seventeenth Century* by Richard Foster Jones and others with the permission of the publishers, Stanford University Press. "William Collins's *Ode on the Death of Thomson*" was a talk on the Third Programme, published in *A Review of English Literature*, July 1960. "Scott's Linguistic Vagaries" was published in *Etudes Anglaises*, April—June 1958. "Thomas Love Peacock" was a lecture given to a joint meeting of the Graduate English Club of the University of Toronto and the Toronto branch of the Humanities Association of Canada, 1955. "The Origins of English Anti-Romanticism" was a paper read to The Oxford University English Club, 1951. "Conrad's *Secret Agent* Reconsidered" was published in *Essays in Criticism*, July 1961; "Is a New History of Criticism Possible?" in the *Cambridge Journal*, June 1949; "*A Mirror for Magistrates* Revisited" in *Elizabethan and Jacobean Studies*, presented to F. P. Wilson, 1959 (Clarendon Press); "Two Ways of Learning" in the *Times Literary Supplement*, 1 October 1954, under the title of "Knowing in Part"; "Research in the Humanities" in the *Yale Review* for 1948; "Lilies or Dandelions?" in the *Cambridge Review*, 12 November 1955; "On Annotating

Paradise Lost IX and X for Schools" in the *Journal of English and Germanic Philology*, Milton number, in honour of Harris Francis Fletcher, October 1961.

May I here thank all those concerned for permission to reprint?

E. M. W. T.

LITERARY

The Nature of Comedy and Shakespeare

I HAVE explained my conception of the literary kinds in the first pages of my *Epic Strain in the English Novel* and I shall do so again in my accompanying essay (pp. 71 ff.) on *The Literary Kinds and Milton*. All I need say here as a preface to remarks on the *genre* of comedy is that any theory of the *genres* likely to mean anything today must associate them with permanent habits of the mind. There was a time when, as operant centres of convention or as sets of rules, they meant a great deal; but as such they are now dead. But if the elegy, for instance, can be regarded not as something convention demands should be written in a certain metre but as the expression of a recognisable human instinct it stands some chance of convincing a modern of its right to exist. It is on such a premiss that I shall discuss the literary kind of comedy.

There is a second premiss on which one finds oneself acting as one would not have done thirty years ago. At that time I should in all likelihood have assumed that among several notions of comedy there was one which, on reflection, turned out to be the right one. Since then we have been subjected to theories of ambiguity, and of multiple meanings imprisoned in a single word, and have learnt to alter our expectations. We now expect that the word *Comedy* when closely inspected will yield more than one meaning, will contain within itself elements referring to different parts of the human mind. And we shall not be disappointed. Here are some of the elements of what conventionally passes for Comedy.

We have been told fairly often that Comedy should be put in terms of the urge to laugh. And it is true that most successful comedies move us to laughter a number of times. But the division of Comedy that makes laughter the principal thing has been called Farce and had better be kept apart from the other divisions.

Two further divisions of Comedy are suggested by the word Picaresque. This should mean a story about a rogue, but in practice it divides itself cleanly into two, exploiting two mental facts. The first, and less important, is sympathy with the underdog, the little man, combined of course with a flattering awareness of our own superiority. He must not be an utter failure, but he must be not quite so well placed as the average, he must have his adventures and must just, and only just, survive them. One of the picaresque heroes in this mode was called Brer Rabbit and another Good Soldier Schweik. And Charlie Chaplin re-embodied him in several films. The other mental fact to be included is both more important and truer to the meaning of the term Picaresque; it is the desire to shed the burdens of duty to self and society without paying too severe a price. In its richest, most serious, form the Picaresque not only rejoices in evading duty but recognises, perhaps ruefully, that you cannot get away with it for ever, that holidays are holidays only because they end, that mankind has after all to toe the line, and that duty has the last word. This perennial pull between evasion and duty has been the subject of a brilliant essay by the late George Orwell in *Horizon*, called the *Art of Donald McGill*. He points out that, while there is one part of you that wishes to be a hero or a saint there is another part of you that is

> a little fat man who sees very clearly the advantages of staying alive with a whole skin. He is your unofficial self, the voice of the belly protesting against the soul. He it is who punctures your fine attitudes and urges you to look after Number One, to be unfaithful to your wife, to bilk your debts. . . . Yet the high sentiments win in the end; leaders who offer blood, toil, tears, and sweat always get more out of their followers than those who offer safety and a good time.

One of the problems of this richer kind of the Picaresque is how to contrive the transition from evasion back to duty. It must have the reader's or spectator's support when it presents evasion but it must also persuade him in due course that evasion has had a long enough innings and that duty must now reassert itself. The most triumphant solution I know of this most difficult and delicate problem occurs not in a play but in a novel: in that supreme picaresque romance, Thackeray's *Vanity Fair*. It is a pity that the author ever called it a novel without a hero, for he thereby encouraged the reader to think of it as something formless or at least to discourage analysis and a definite judgement. We had better ignore Thackeray's addendum and remember that his only full-length novel that preceded *Vanity Fair* was *Barry Lyndon*. Now *Barry Lyndon*, whatever the virtues of its parts, is a simple and even rather crude example of the picaresque narrative. It presents the adventures of a bad man; and his badness is so obvious and unmixed that we have no great sympathy with his gambles and his hazards. In other words, Thackeray fails here to exploit to the full the universal human desire that George Orwell described so well; he fails, as the best writers of picaresque should not do, to put us for the time being on the side of the rogue or adventurer. His rogue is ultimately unsuccessful in the necessary manner, but with no more subtle contrivance than that he should fail to impose any longer and end up in prison. The result is that the novel makes no clear total impression and exists for the pleasure of the mere narrative and of the scarce-connected incidents. Having created one, imperfect, picaresque narrative, no wonder if Thackeray in his next venture sought to follow it by a better. Perhaps I should not say "sought" as if he admitted to what he was doing. Rather he followed his true instincts in making Becky Sharp his picaresque heroine with her husband Rawdon Crawley only a little below her as a kind of hero-consort. Though Thackeray indeed followed his true instincts he would not own up to them but christened his work a novel without a hero. Becky and Rawdon are both adventurers and for a while they join in preying on society; and for a while, indeed for more than half the book, we are mostly on their side, wishing them luck. Nor do these wishes represent a mere crude desire of ours to be grossly lawless. Becky had the virtue of courage and the excuse of poverty and a hard childhood, not shared by any of the book's main characters. So we too have our excuse for sympathising with her in a way unjustifiable on strictly moral grounds. Here is a situation altogether richer and subtler than that existing in *Barry Lyndon*. Another excuse for sympathising with Becky and Rawdon is that they are not the only adventurers. Old Osborne is the successful adventurer in business; the self-made man. Joe Sedley, timid as he is, adventures for money in India. Young Osborne is the *parvenu* among the aristocrats who then held most of the commissions in the British army. Many of the characters are or have been on the make and they unite to give the novel its special character. The disinterestedness of Dobbin and Amelia is a smaller affair and serves as a foil rather than forms the main substance. Like Shakespeare in *Henry IV*, Thackeray had the problem of cutting short his picaresque protagonist's career of success and he solved it brilliantly. He makes Rawdon turn into a less unscrupulous and more decent character as he grows into middle age, and largely through his affection for the son for whom his wife has no use. In fact, Thackeray breaks up the alliance between the two chief adventurers and forces us to distribute our sympathies. While still admiring Becky's courage we find ourselves dwelling as never before on her callousness and we end by acquiescing in her downfall. It is wonderful with what insensible smoothness Thackeray induces us to make this great change of feeling. Then, after this change, he has the equally difficult task of making more sympathetic the two virtuous characters whose virtue must so far be kept from being too engaging less it usurp the preponderance of our sympathy; and he does so by introducing a bit of selfishness into the hitherto annoyingly unselfish Amelia—that is when she begins to make a slave of Dobbin —and by introducing a bit of spirit and pride into Dobbin when he ultimately revolts against her tyranny. By the time the book ends we have forgiven the two the very patent defects of their virtues and accept them, perhaps with a bit of a sigh but none the less surely, as symbols of that duty from which the adventurers have persuaded us temporarily to escape.

Walter Allen, impressed by the breadth and diversity of the scene of *Vanity Fair*, said that the only analogue was *War and Peace* and proceeded to damn the former for not standing up to the comparison. The analogue is false, and its falseness came from confusing two different literary kinds. *War and Peace* is of the epic kind, and if you judge *Vanity Fair* as an epic it fails. Judged as a picaresque narrative it comes as near success as most great works of art are likely to do.

Queerer things than the Picaresque can be included in the vast range of so-called Comedy. Take the earliest of Chapman's comedies, the *Blind Beggar of Alexandria*. It survives in a truncated form, but its nature is clear enough. The hero, Cleanthes, low-born and a climber like Marlowe's Tamburlaine, brings a wild and romantic heroic action to a happy conclusion. But he also conducts a separate comic action in the disguise of a blind beggar, assumed because in his own person he has been banished the land. This action consists in his assuming further disguises and, thus disguised, in courting and marrying three sisters in succession. Having done this, he proceeds to cuckold himself by re-courting his wives in a different disguise and thus appearing to seduce them. T. M. Parrott, Chapman's editor, considers this comic action "an absurd and coarse farce." But it was greatly to the taste of the Elizabethan audience and accounted for the popularity of the play. For myself I find nothing coarse about the extravagance of the comic action but instead a charming airiness of fantasy; and the kind of pleasure I get from it resembles what I get from *Zuleika Dobson*. If the Picaresque in its richest form gives you the forsaking and the resuming of duty, such fantasy provides a holiday from all the normal conditions of life. Psychologically, though often included in the comic, it is as remote as can be from what is usually taken to be the characteristic area of Comedy, to which I now turn.

As an enormous and rough generalisation one can say that Tragedy concerns man's relations to the sum of things, Comedy his relations to his neighbour or society. Comedy assumes that society must be made to work, that creatures must somehow learn to live together. It is a very old doctrine; older than man. Len Howard in her book, *Living with Birds*, describes the social laws under which birds have agreed to live. Occasionally they break them; and the chief offender in her own observation was a female blackbird she had named Star. And she comments, "If every bird acted like Star, there would be pandemonium in their nesting affairs." So even among birds society must assert itself; and human comedy had to do with this fundamental assertion. Alter the name of Star to Katherina and then cause her to conform to the laws of society, and you find yourself in the centre of the comic norm.

Within this norm you can distribute the emphasis differently. A writer can be positive and therefore probably genial. He can show people behaving as he thinks they ought to behave in society. He can show a Portia living up to her principles of mercy and good will. Or he can present the spectacle of a man or men at odds with society, through either absurdity or crime, and of how they are brought to heel. He can present young men, pretending they can do without women for several years, shown up for what they are worth, or a humourless man, inflated in self-importance as a steward in a rich house, thinking he can reduce others to his own narrow and gloomy standards and being punished. Or he can go farther towards satire and show a bad man offending seriously against society until at last he is found out and thwarted.

Nevill Coghill in a stimulating article in the *Essays and Studies of the English Association* entitled the *Basis of Shakespearean Comedy* distinguishes sharply between these two kinds and proceeds to link the medieval comic spirit (inherited by Shakespeare) with the positive, genial kind, and Classical comedy and its Italian progeny (adopted by Ben Jonson) with the negative or satirical kind. There is some truth in the distinctions, but I think Coghill makes them neater than in fact they are. For instance there is a bigger range in Classical comedy than he allows. The *Rudens* of Plautus, with its romantic marine setting, its kindly middle-aged chief character who ends by forgiving the villain and asking him to dinner, is nearer to Shakespeare than to Jonson. Nevertheless, coming as I now do to Shakespeare, I admit that his comedy does not extend far in the direction of the didactic and the satiric. He may mock at fools, pedants and braggarts, but he does not make it a habit to denounce bad men. But if he limits himself on that side, in every other way he is opulent, exploiting all the parts of the mind to which I have tried to refer in this essay.

II. SHAKESPEARE

What distinguishes Shakespeare's comedies from most contemporary ones is the amount of blending. Each play is sharply individualised, and yet nearly every one contains in different proportions all the elements of the others.

Take the play that is the most concerned with the sheer provocation of laughter, the *Comedy of Errors*. Here by complicating his originals through the addition of a second pair of twins Shakespeare mounts to a region of fantasy beyond the scope of ordinary farce. At the same time he makes his social setting real in a way that is unnecessary for the purely farcical effect. In the midst of wild hilarity the question of how fallible mortals are to live together makes itself felt. Adriana, the wife of Antipholus of Ephesus, is a stupid woman who fusses over her husband, while her sister Luciana is brighter and more worldly-wise. When, mistakenly, Luciana thinks that her brother-in-law is making love to her she is mindful of what Jane Austen called the duty of woman to woman and seeks to shield her sister from the consequences of the threatened infidelity by telling Antipholus of Syracuse (mistaken for the other) that at least he must pretend affection for his wife:

> If you did wed my sister for her wealth,
> Then for her wealth's sake use her with more kindness;
> Or, if you like elsewhere, do it by stealth;
> Muffle your false love with some show of blindness.
>
> 'Tis double wrong to truant with your bed
> And let her read it in thy looks at board;
> Shame hath a bastard fame, well managed;
> Ill deeds is doubled with an evil word.

Then, gentle brother, get you in again;
Comfort my sister, cheer her, call her wife.
'Tis holy sport to be a little vain,
When the sweet breath of flattery conquers strife.

Later Adriana, believing her husband to be mad, tries to
force an entry into the priory where he has gone for refuge
and take him back home, for she thinks in her stupidity that
she is the only woman who can deal with him and nurse him
back to health. Then the Lady Abbess appears and plays a
rather cruel trick on the poor woman, rather cruel but not
undeserved. This is the passage:

Abb. Hath he not lost much wealth by wreck of sea?
        Buried some dear friend? Hath not else his eye
        Strayed his affection in unlawful love?
        Which of these sorrows is he subject to?
Adr. To none of these except it be the last;
        Namely, some love that drew him oft from home.
Abb. You should for that have reprehended him.
Adr. Why, so I did.
Abb.   Ay, but not rough enough.
Adr. As roughly as my modesty would let me.
Abb. Haply in private.
Adr.   And in assemblies too.
Abb. Ay, but not enough.
Adr. It was the copy of our conference.
        In bed, he slept not for my urging it;
        At board, he fed not for my urging it;
        Alone, it was the subject of my theme;
        In company, I often glanced at it;
        Still I did tell him it was vile and bad.
Abb. And thereof came it that the man was mad.
        The venom clamours of a jealous woman
        Poisons more deadly than a mad dog's tooth.

And the Abbess spends sixteen more lines in rubbing this
truth in. Whereupon Luciana can stand her silly sister's
humiliation no longer but breaks in with

> She never reprehended him but mildly,
> When he demean'd himself rough, rude, and wildly.
> Why bear you these rebukes and answer not?

This dialogue has nothing to do with the farce; if it makes us laugh it does so in a much less uproarious way than the confusion caused by mistaken identities. In fact it belongs to the central social area of comedy, helping to turn farce into something richer than its simple and exaggerated self.

Shakespeare wrote no play of the picaresque kind I mentioned first. He never made the underdog the main character. But in play after play through the clowns, the servants, and the fools he makes us aware of him. "Truly, sir," says Pompey to Escalus in *Measure for Measure*, "I am a poor fellow that would live." The plays are full of such poor fellows, and Shakespeare sees to it that somehow they shall live. Even Parolles in *All's Well*, in spite of the damage he has done, once he has been unmasked and reduced to the status of poor fellow, is not allowed to go under. Lafeu, who ruined him as adventurer, will make use of him as poor fellow;

> Sirrah, inquire further after me; I had talk of you last night.
> Though you are a fool and a knave, you shall eat. Go to; follow.

The other kind of Picaresque Shakespeare exploited more obviously, and through the person of Falstaff. Among the things that Falstaff represents must certainly be "the voice of the belly protesting against the soul." Further he persuades us to be on the side of that protest. And further still his creator meant us to change sides towards the end of the second of the two plays in which the authentic Falstaff figures. Thus Shakespeare was trying to do the same kind of thing that Thackeray did in *Vanity Fair*. All agree that he triumphs as long as he wants us to be on Falstaff's side and to hope that he gets away with his gambles. But not all think that he succeeds in transferring our allegiance, in making us agree that it is time for justice to assert itself and for the rascal to get his due reward. The way you feel on this old controversy depends on how far you allow your head to intervene in the promptings of the heart, and perhaps too on how

far you can put yourself in the place of Shakespeare's contemporaries. Thackeray secured his difficult transfer of
loyalty by working on our hearts, by making us fond of
Rawdon in a way we had not been before, and, in consequence, by arousing our resentment when Becky betrays
him. Shakespeare does nothing of this kind with Justice
Shallow, whom Falstaff deceives shortly before his fall. He is
his old foolish and vain self when he appears for the last time,
and we are rather pleased than not that he should throw
away a thousand pounds on the picaresque adventurer. On
the other hand, when, on the old king's death, Falstaff says
he will double-charge Pistol with dignities and make Justice
Shallow Lord Shallow, we must know, unless we are far gone
in sentimentalism, that Falstaff has overreached himself and
that his day is over. Our minds force us into the realm of
duty. Where Shakespeare's contemporaries would differ
from ourselves in their conception of Falstaff is in the quality
of their commitment to him. However warmly committed,
they would know all the time, in a way not easy for us to
grasp, that Falstaff stood for disorder from the beginning
and that they must be prepared all through and at any time
for his downfall.

Here let me interpose the commonplace that Falstaff in
the *Merry Wives of Windsor* is no longer the picaresque
adventurer with whom one sympathises over a great part of
the action; adding that it is grossly unfair to Shakespeare to
suggest that in any way he ought to be. I conjecture that
Shakespeare would simply not have begun to understand the
notion that he was obliged to keep Falstaff consistent. With
the most obvious part of himself he welcomed Falstaff as a
popular success; with a less obvious part he was glad to have
expressed certain motions of his mind through him. But the
idea of Falstaff as a creation to which he must at all costs be
loyal was outside his ken. The sacrosanctity of Falstaff was a
late development, hardly begun in Dryden's day; and in his
hurry to make another play in which Falstaff had to figure
Shakespeare had not the least scruple in making the nominal
Falstaff serve whatever turn happened to suit him. To be
fair, then, you must acquiesce in what Shakespeare lets us

know very quickly by the whole tone of his writing: that this Falstaff *is* a different man. The critics who refuse to acquiesce turn the play into a far worse affair than it actually is. I admit that they have a grain or two of excuse, for Shakespeare was unguarded and inconsistent enough to allow a few touches of the old Falstaff to confuse his new character. These touches are confined to Falstaff's own account of being tipped with the foul linen into the Thames.

> And then, to be stopp'd in like a strong distillation, with stinking clothes that fretted in their own grease. Think of that—a man of my kidney. Think of that—that am as subject to heat as butter; a man of continual dissolution and thaw. It was a miracle to scape suffocation. And in the height of this bath, when I was more than half-stew'd in grease, like a Dutch dish, to be thrown into the Thames and cool'd, glowing hot, in that surge, like a horseshoe; think of that—hissing hot. Think of that, Master Brook.

That is the old Falstaff, quite in command of the situation, telling a story against himself just because he is so sure that he can afford to do so. You can say with superficial plausibility that this with the rest of Falstaff's account is the best thing in the play; but if you do, you sacrifice almost the whole to a very small part. It is both more true and fairer to Shakespeare to call these passages blemishes, alienating us from the rest of the play, and to give them as little attention as we can contrive. Treated thus, the *Merry Wives* is a better play than is usually allowed: an excellent, if lightly felt and unsubtle, social comedy; less complicated and more conventional than any other of Shakespeare's plays but beautifully contrived within its limits. It contains more farce than any play outside the *Comedy of Errors*, but its sphere is the social norm, set principally by the Pages with their general good sense. Against this norm Falstaff is the principal offender, and we never have the least sympathy with his offences. Even the Pages offend against the norm they are the means of setting when they try to marry their daughter to unsuitable men; and they have to be brought to heel. Though committed but shallowly in his emotions, Shakespeare plotted the play beautifully, spread an air of geniality through the prose that he used for most of the play, and introduced verse with great skill towards the end: verse serving to give variety, to support the more romantic interest of Anne Page's secret wedding, and to prepare for the heightened fantasy of Falstaff's final humiliation in the darkness of Windsor Park.

The casual occurrence of fantasy in the *Merry Wives*, even if it is fantasy contrived by persons in the play and is not that of the author's own mood, suggests that the kind of fantasy which I have described as sometimes included in things called comedies, and have illustrated from Chapman's *Blind Beggar of Alexandria*, is an incidental quality; and the suggestion is true. Fantasy so airy and unattached as Chapman's never constitutes a main motive in Shakespeare's comedies. The fairy scenes in *A Midsummer Night's Dream* contain too much of the rational and are too firmly integrated with the rest of the play to be fantasy of that sort. We must go rather to minor flights, like Launce's account of the extreme measures to which he resorted in defence of his dog, for a true comparison. A remark that leads to the digression that the play in which Launce and his dog occur is the only play of those hitherto not discussed from among the early and middle comedies (my proper theme) that has not for its norm the way people live together, man's duty to his neighbour. The *Two Gentlemen of Verona* cannot be classified; it evades all the propensities of the mind that I have held to enter the literary kind of Comedy. Proteus is too unpleasant a man to arouse the degree of sympathy we may dare to give to the normal picaresque adventurer. The climax of the play with Proteus's capture and exposure, his frivolously sudden repentance leading to Valentine's equally frivolous surrender of his true love, Silvia, to his friend, belongs to a world of the most rarefied and abstract conventions and not to the world of men; and Shakespeare fails to reduce it to absurdity by matching it with real life. There is much interesting or exciting or beautiful detail, but the only steady feelings I can detect in the play have to do with sheer technique. Shakespeare rejoices in the skill with which he conducts the plot and the strength with which he carries a big scene through. An example of this strength can be found in the first 185 lines of the third act, where Proteus betrays to the Duke Valentine's plan to elope with Silvia; and the Duke, catching Valentine with a rope ladder concealed under his cloak, sends him into banishment. No writer of the time other than Shakespeare could have made the episode so ample and yet so swift and significant. It is massive without sacrificing a scrap of vitality.

In the great comedies of Shakespeare's early and middle years, before he wrote the so-called Problem Plays, there may be hints of the tragedies to come, of a concern with man faced by the sum of things; but preponderatingly they belong to the central and typical area of Comedy. However much Shakespeare may stray from it into farce, fantasy, or melodrama, he comes to rest in the social norm; he is first interested in the way men get on together. Even in so stylised a play as *Love's Labour's Lost*, where the theme is as much the words men use as the lives they lead, he comes to rest in the norm of everyday life, and specially of the country life that in those days preponderated in England, with the shepherds piping in spring and the girls bleaching their frocks against the summer and in winter the coughing in church and Tom bearing logs into the hall of the great house. Incidentally, it was an astonishing stroke of art to convey something so crucial to the play's totality in two lyrics that have charmed myriads simply as lyrics, in detachment.

Even *Romeo and Juliet* betrays Shakespeare's interest at this time in the social life. It is a difficult play to judge sanely; for calf-love is a heady brew, and it is hard not to allow the scenes of courtship and fruition and parting to get out of proportion. I suspect that their headiness has prevented the generality of readers from giving due praise to the massive and unstinted evolution of the plot. Shakespeare himself was far from allowing the love scenes to upset his sense of proportion. Further, he fitted them beautifully into a larger social setting. The Capulet mansion is full of bustling life from the supper near the beginning to the abortive wedding feast near the end, as when a servant bursts into the room where Lady Capulet, Julia, and the Nurse are talking with:

> Madam, the guests are come, supper serv'd up, you call'd, my young lady ask'd for, the nurse curs'd in the pantry, and everything in extremity. I must hence to wait; I beseech you follow straight.

And the splendid opening scene with the street-brawl of the rival houses is a thoroughly domestic affair shared by gentry and servants. It is a commonplace that the tragic quality of *Romeo and Juliet* is unlike that of the mature tragedies. It does not provoke thought about man's relation with the sum of things; we exclaim rather that the couple have had a grand run for their money even if they become the victims of bad luck at the end. And if there is a moral it is a social one: "look what happens in a society when things get out of hand." Thus *Romeo and Juliet* is closer than one first thinks to the comedies that were occupying Shakespeare at this time.

The preponderant tone of *A Midsummer Night's Dream* and of *The Merchant of Venice* is one of positive goodwill, setting forth charity in action in the commonwealth, and indeed in the first of these through the universe. Everything leads to an embracing harmony. Shakespeare's final phase before the Problem Plays was more critical though always on this side of positive satire. His verse and prose reach a flexible beauty unknown before; and it is the mixture of enchanting beauty with the critical spirit that constitutes these plays' peculiar excellence.

Much Ado about Nothing, *As You Like It*, and *Twelfth Night* are commonly regarded as Shakespeare's highest reach in the norm of comedy; and I see no reason to challenge this regard. But *Twelfth Night* is not so sure of itself as comedy and may also be on the way to something else. The other two are companion pieces. They are alike in showing the critical spirit in fullest activity; they differ in the way they apply that spirit to society. Both of course continue the manifestation of positive good will, just mentioned, along with developing the critical spirit. In *Much Ado* (to strip the play to its barest bones) Shakespeare tells us that it is wise to recognise the illogicality and the ineptitude of happenings in human society; if you expect anything else you will be disappointed and pay the penalty for your blindness. And Shakespeare embodies his theme by making grave intentions miscarry and trivial causes work important ends. To achieve the greatest emphasis this theme must include the grandiose; hence the melodramatic scene in church when the principal lady is denounced as unchaste and the expected marriage is abandoned. But the big scene already lacks its point, and for more than one reason. First, the principal man, Claudio, and the principal woman, Hero, are not the chief personalities; they are not the people who fitly and logically should be subjected to the most searching experiences. Second, the misapprehension under which Claudio acts must very soon be cleared up— it is a matter of a mere hour or two—because the truth has been revealed in another but adjacent quarter. Claudio's unnecessary denunciation arouses superfluous passions in the remaining principal characters, and all the pains that they take to clear up the trouble are superfluous because the fantastic incompetence of Dogberry and his men has anticipated by a fluke the carefully directed efforts of their betters. "What your wisdoms could not discover these shallow fools have brought to light." The two persons with the greatest underlying force of character, Benedick and Beatrice, figure primarily in the very unserious and unmelodramatic subplot. In it they fall victims to a simple strategem which less intelligent people might have detected more readily. And the strategem itself may have been superfluous in view of the covert attraction the two sprightly bickerers had for each other.

If in *Much Ado* all sorts of things are superfluous and cancel out, in *As You Like It* nothing cancels out and all combinations are possible; through it Shakespeare tells us that under the law of charity and through the exercise of steady wisdom most things can be fitted into life without conflicting. I will take a single passage as a paradigm. In the play's original, Lodge's *Rosalind*, Aliena thus charges Ganimede with abusing the privilege of her masculine disguise to blacken her sex:

> And I pray you, quoth Aliena, if your robes were off, what metal are you made of that you are so satirical against women? Is it not a foul bird defiles his own nest?

Shakespeare remembered the passage and transformed it by making Celia say to Rosalind:

> You have simply misused our sex in your love-prate: we must have your doublet and hose plucked over your head and show the world what the bird hath done to her own nest.

If you begin thinking about this passage you can only conclude that it is outrageous; there may even be a glance (of infinitesimal duration) at the gruesome account of the stripping and showing up of Duessa near the end of the first book of the *Faerie Queene*: and we may remark that Dr. Thomas Bowdler in his *Family Shakespeare*, having, rather surprisingly, let through "have your doublet and hose plucked over your head," drew the line at the rest. And yet in reading the passage or hearing it on the stage our first thought is of the perfect elegance of Celia's expression. But elegance does not suppress outrage: on the contrary the two things co-exist in full development yet in perfect peace, the elegance disinfecting the outrage, and the outrage giving the elegance a tang. Rosalind herself confirms this peaceful co-existence of apparent opposites, combining the utmost warmth of affection with the utmost coolness of the critical spirit, brought to bear largely on herself. By his title Shakespeare asked us to take things easy, to take these combinations as you like them provided you let their constituent parts live. And we may be sure that, as Shakespeare liked, all the elements of all the combinations should be fulfilled simultaneously. In spite of its apparent ease no play of Shakespeare includes more or masters its content more magnificently. It is his supreme demonstration of how the process of living in society can, by the exercise of charity and wisdom, by warmth of heart and coolness of head, compass a surprising and splendid richness of content.

What then is our conclusion? Two things the very reverse of sensational. First, the literary kind of comedy covers several countries of the human mind, even if it is most at home in one of these, namely that concerned with the adjustment of the individual to society. Second, Shakespeare includes all these countries in his range, reaching his maturest art in dealing with that country where the literary kind called comedy is most at home.

The Trial Scene in "The Merchant of Venice"

MRS JAMESON declared that in the trial scene Portia had two objects in view: to deliver her husband's friend and to maintain her husband's honour by the discharge of his just debt. "It is evident that she would owe the safety of Antonio to anything rather than to the legal quibble with which her cousin Bellario has armed her, and which she reserves as a last resource." I wonder. Was the legal quibble a last, and presumably uncertain, resource? or is Mrs Jameson, through the very definiteness of her error, suggesting an equally definite contrary embodying a truth not yet fully apprehended? May not the legal quibble be, not a last resource, but a trump-card Portia keeps serenely up her sleeve while transacting business quite other than that which Mrs Jameson assigns to her? The moment Portia produces her quibble, Shylock's case collapses. His enemies know instantaneously that it has collapsed, and he attempts not a single quibble in retort. In its context the quibble is an infallible magic spell, in keeping with the fairy-tale substance of the two main plots. If the ghost of Mrs Jameson objected that Portia, having the saving spell, would surely have used it without delay, it can be answered that Shakespeare postponed its use for the reason why Thackeray denied Joe Sedley the chance of proposing to Becky Sharp: that he did not choose to cut short what he had in mind to write. If, says Thackeray, Joe had proposed to Becky, his novel would not have been written.

What then was it that Shakespeare most had to say, granted that his Portia was untroubled in mind on Antonio's account, knowing that she possessed a spell insuring his release? As a practising dramatist he wanted in the first place to present an effective scene, something of the greatest possible dramatic interest; and indeed it is an enrichment of the dramatic situation if Portia knows she has Shylock quite within her power while the other characters are in the dark;

if she is cool about the thing all the others agonise over; if she is tempted to prolong her moment of power before enjoying the supreme satisfaction of giving to the sorely tried sufferers their unexpected and spectacular relief. I would not deny the presence of such elements; only they coexist with much else.

In his *Basis of Shakespearean Comedy*[1] Nevill Coghill made some important points: that the age of the *Faerie Queene* must have been generally expectant of allegory; that some of Shakespeare's comedies demand figurative as well as natural-istic understanding; and that the *Merchant of Venice* is among them. He holds that the play repeats the much exploited medieval theme of the conflict of Justice and Mercy, asso-ciating it especially with that stylised form of it, the legend of the Four Daughters of God. These, Pity Truth Justice Peace, were the virtues of man as first created. At the Fall he lost them, and in their personified form they became the Four Daughters of God. Truth and Justice were man's accusers, Pity (or Mercy) and Peace his advocates. Through Christ's agency the four were reconciled: "Mercy and Truth are met together; Justice and Peace have kissed each other." The legend, having entered the Morality Play, was part of the medieval inheritance of the Elizabethan age. Coghill considers the conflict between Shylock and Antonio an *exemplum* of the traditional theme. While not accepting some of the details of Coghill's account, I think he gives a neces-sary general truth about the play. But also I think he does not see the full part Portia has in the conflict between Justice and Mercy.

The *Merchant of Venice* belongs to the years when Spen-ser's vogue was at its height, when any educated audience would be familiar with Spenser's habit of sliding characters along a scale that was naturalistic at one end and allegorical at the other; his most elaborate example being that of Mal-becco, who, from being a highly realistic jealous old man, turns into a perfected allegory of Jealousy. Having seen Portia begin as a witty Elizabethan lady, change into the

[1] *Essays and Studies of the English Association*, 1950, pp. 1-28.

fairy-princess of the Beautiful Mountain, and change again into the tom-boy of contemporary romantic comedy, the original audience would have been well prepared for further changes. Moreover, in the Trial Scene, she enters doubly disguised, as a man and as a doctor of laws of Rome; hence the readier to have exchanged an old for a new self. She arrives in state, heralded by a forerunner, and her tone, when she has entered, is magisterial. She dictates what is right or wrong and speaks with more authority than the Duke himself; while Bassanio assumes that she can "wrest the law" of Venice itself to her will. She has ceased to be a young woman and has turned into an allegory—of what? Not of Mercy alone, though that is her main theme, and though the audience, knowing her to be a woman and mindful of Spenser's Mercilla, would at once be prone to take her as such. But she is Mercy clothed in the robes of Justice and can only stand for Justice and Mercy reconciled, in accordance with her own words about earthly power being most godlike "when mercy seasons justice." Mercy must season justice but may not "wrest" it, and Bassanio's plea can only be rejected.

We have arrived at this point, then, that Portia stands for Mercy reconciled with Justice and that she knows she possesses the infallible means of rescuing Antonio according to the strict letter of justice, Antonio not needing in actual fact any exercise of mercy at all. But Christian mercy is not confined to the plight of a single unfortunate Venetian; it is concerned with the souls of all men, specifically here of Jews as well as of Venetians. Thus, when Portia lectures Shylock on mercy, while the other persons on the stage can only think of Antonio's fate, she is thinking of Shylock's, she is imploring Shylock to recognise his own peril and to mind the salvation of his own soul. And that is the second reason why Shakespeare prolongs the scene; he must allow due scope for Portia's plea. If we read the scene on these lines we shall see that it gains greatly in richness of content.

Let me now examine the scene (IV, 1) in the light of what I have written. It begins with the utter lack of mercy in

Shylock, who is "void and empty/From any dram of mercy," and with Antonio's recognition of this and consequent resignation of spirit. Even so the Duke, who has thus characterised Shylock, does not give up all hope but tells Shylock on his entry that he still expects a change of mood in him at the eleventh hour. So far, all our thoughts are directed towards Antonio or towards Shylock only so far as his mood affects Antonio. And when Shylock enlarges on his abhorrence of his debtor and on his inflexibility he confirms that direction. Then, for the first time, with the Duke's words, "How shalt thou hope for mercy, rendering none?" we are reminded of Shylock's soul. Shylock, insensitive to this Christian plea, asserts that he has nothing to fear, for he has the law on his side; and he begins to stand for Legality as well as retaining his human character. The Duke can now do no more for Antonio, and the last, slender chance is the opinion of the lawyer, Bellario, whom the Duke has consulted by letter and whose messenger is at hand. Again, with Bassanio's "Good cheer, Antonio; what, man, courage yet!" it is Antonio's fate alone we think of. And yet, a few lines after, Gratiano glances at the other theme with his "Not on thy sole but on thy soul, harsh Jew,/Thou makst thy knife keen." But he only glances, for when he proceeds to abuse Shylock for his brutality he has removed the word *soul* from its Christian context and made it mean no more than *disposition:*

> thy currish spirit
> Governed a wolf, who, hanged for human slaughter,
> Even from the gallows did his fell soul fleet
> And, whilst thou layst in thy unhallowed dam,
> Infused itself in thee.

Thus, when Portia enters, our attention is mainly fixed on Antonio's predicament. For all that, if we have listened properly, we should have some awareness of the peril in which Shylock's soul stands, faint perhaps but ready to be roused by further reference.

The Portia who enters is, as I have said, magisterial, quite altered from the young girl whose little body was aweary of this great world. She also goes headlong into action unlike both the lovesick girl who wished to detain Bassanio "some month or two" before undergoing that other judgement of the caskets and the procrastinating Venetians among whom she finds herself. She is like a cold draught of air suddenly penetrating a hot room and refreshing the wits of those within. Both by her difference and by her fresh energy she leads us to expect a novel way of feeling. It takes her only a moment to find that Antonio acknowledges his obligation to his bond: upon which she tells Shylock he must be merciful; Shylock queries her *must*; and she begins her oration on mercy. How does this speech satisfy the audience's expectation of the novel way of feeling I have just postulated? First, it defines the change in Portia's nature. If she is now magisterial and more certain of herself than the other characters on the stage, it is because she has a new dignity as embodying that mercy on which she expatiates. Second, her speech attaches itself to formal rhetoric in a way none of the previous speeches in the scene have done. As Margaret Schlauch has recently written:

> Portia's great plea for mercy is in a sense the culmination of many exercises on this theme, extending from ancient times down to the sixteenth century. . . . The opportunity to elaborate *colores* upon the noble theme of mercy may well have been one of the most important rhetorical factors causing Shakespeare to make use of the improbable plot about Shylock's bond.[1]

And we accept this new rhetoric just because we have been startled by the nature of Portia's entry. But, thirdly, we should also perceive that the speech must be interpreted with a richness of reference not belonging to anything that has gone before but not unexpected in view of the jolt to which we have been submitted.

Take the actual text of the speech, and it is plain that Portia's plea for mercy concerns both Shylock's soul and Antonio's life: mercy is twice blest, benefiting both giver and

[1] In *Kwartalnik Neofilologiczny* (Warsaw) for 1960, *Roman "Controversiae" and the Court Scene in Shakespeare's "Merchant of Venice"*, p. 56.

receiver. And Portia tells Shylock, Christianwise, that justice alone is insufficient for the soul's salvation. But the mere text becomes greatly complicated through the different ways the characters take it. The Duke, having already referred to Shylock's soul, must surely give at least a passing thought to it when Portia dwells so insistently on the benefit mercy brings its giver. But the other Venetians, bent so intently on poor Antonio's plight, value her words solely as they are likely to persuade Shylock to soften and so to spare his victim. Portia, knowing Antonio to be safe, aims all her eloquence at Shylock and Shylock alone. Shylock, obsessed with his hate, is deaf to the tones of her entreaty and has not the remotest idea that she pleads essentially for him and his welfare, that she is fulfilling the command of Christ to love your enemy. The audience knew the outlines of the story, knew that Antonio would not in fact lose his pound of flesh; but would not thereby be prevented (any more than in witnessing *Oedipus King* or *Othello*) from being caught up in the excitement of the plot, from experiencing the supposed tension of the persons in the story while the issue is undecided. At the same time they should recognise the other issue and watch Portia in her struggle to break down Shylock's obtuseness, ready to take her words both in the way she means them and in the way the Venetians (the Duke perhaps excepted) do in fact take them. The audience are thus in a wonderfully happy position: ironically superior to most persons in the play by possessing additional knowledge and thrilled by the excitement of having two parallel meanings to apprehend. For illustration, take the way Portia begins the action:

Por.   Do you confess the bond?
Ant.   I do.
Por.   Then must the Jew be merciful.
Shy.   On what compulsion must I? Tell me that.
Por.   The quality of mercy is not strained.

Here in the second line the Venetians take Portia to mean that Antonio's only (and therefore crucial) chance of life is Shylock's relenting. Portia means that Shylock cannot escape the risk of a mortal sin through some lucky flaw in the operation of the bond which will save him from the responsibility of claiming his pound of flesh, and that it is imperative for his soul's sake that he should even yet be merciful. When Shylock queries Portia's *must*, the Venetians accept his query and hope that Portia's eloquence will sway him to spare Antonio. Portia, having first said *must* and then said that there are no *musts* about mercy, tries to stir Shylock's set and stupid wits. Can't he see that she is using *must* in two different senses? It is of the utmost consequence to you, she means, that you should be merciful; but when it comes to mercy no one can force you, the impulse must come from your own heart, or from the yielding of your heart to the operation of heavenly grace.

And thus the scene proceeds. Seen from the point of view of Portia's Christian pleading, Shylock's retort to her eloquence, "My deeds upon my head," is indeed dreadful in its self-damnation. Unable to convince Shylock of the beauty of mercy in its own right, Portia climbs down from the height from which she has begun and appeals to his advantage with, "Shylock, there's thrice thy money offered thee;" only to find Shylock taking his stand on ground more elevated and yet for his soul's health more perilous than a simple love of gain:

> An oath, an oath, I have an oath in Heaven.
> Shall I lay perjury upon my soul?

Solicitous for his own soul on purely legal premises he cannot begin to see that Portia is also solicitous, but on premises how different! Then Portia repeats both pleas simultaneously, after dwelling on the most dreadful item in the bond: that the flesh to be cut shall be nearest to the heart. Shylock refuses with an emphasis grimmer than before, bringing in his soul yet again:

> by my soul I swear
> There is no power in the tongue of man
> To alter me.

Antonio perceives the emphasis and that Portia has failed; he

asks for an end of the trial. But even as the end appears to
approach, Portia, giving Shylock every chance (or, as the
Venetians think, not abandoning the minutest portion of
hope on behalf of Antonio), implores Shylock to get a
surgeon to stop his victim's bleeding to death, on the Christian plea of charity. And having made this plea in vain Portia
abandons her struggle for Shylock's soul. She is now free to
abandon also her high allegorical role, which she begins to do
when, in comment on Bassanio's protest that his friend's life
is more to him than his own life, wife, and all the world, she
exclaims:

> Your wife would give you little thanks for that,
> If she were by, to hear you make the offer.

Begins, because she has not yet finished with her judicial
part. However, having begun, she must not delay her return
to common humanity too long, as the play must not dwell
too long in solemn things lest it lose its predominantly comic
complexion. So she hastens to produce her trump-card, her
unassailable legal quibble; and the tension, so long sustained,
now breaks. Portia has no concern but with justice against
Shylock; mercy now being the province of the Duke and
Antonio. The Duke is generous, granting Shylock his life in
anticipation of his plea for it, and being willing to commute
confiscation of half his property to a fine. But pardon comes
easier to the Duke than to Shylock's victim; and Portia is
careful to distinguish between them, finally asking what
mercy Antonio can render Shylock. Antonio is on the whole
generous in the matter of money, but he makes the stipulation that Shylock shall turn Christian, a stipulation made
definitive by the Duke, who says he will rescind his pardon
unless Shylock complies.

In interpreting Antonio's stipulation one encounters the
kind of dilemma presented by Hamlet's motives for sparing
Claudius at his prayers and the irreconcilable dispute between
the tough and the tender critics. Everything is so simple if
you can follow the tough ones. These (and on this issue
Coghill is among them) point out that the Elizabethans
thought nothing odd about forcible conversions. Baptism

was necessary for salvation, and it "worked" as surely when forced as when chosen. Thus Antonio performed an act of pure Christian mercy, when, forgoing revenge, he stipulated that Shylock should turn Christian; he was returning good for evil. I should like to get out of the dilemma so easily; but in view of the many cross-references in the play and of the irony I have described as running through the trial scene I cannot help doubting so simple an explanation. Think of these cross-references: can it be fortuitous that Antonio begins the play's first scene with "In sooth I know not why I am so sad:/ It wearies me," and that Portia begins the second scene with "By my troth, Nerissa, my little body is aweary of this great world;" or again can it be fortuitous that over the triviality of the ring Bassanio and Antonio swear on their souls as Shylock had sworn on his soul over the vital matter of his bond? Thus, when Antonio and the Duke in their mercy force Shylock to turn Christian, we are surely meant to recall Portia's pronouncement that you cannot force mercy. Of course the tough critics can argue that Portia's forcing refers to the giver not the receiver of mercy, and that Antonio choosing freely to force mercy on Shylock was acting according to her principles. And yet in my heart I am convinced that Portia included the receiver in her ken and that Shakespeare meant some ironical contrast between Portia's ideals and the cruder standards of the Venetians.

Certainly if he does and if I am right in detecting a long series of double meanings in Portia's speeches, the trial scene comes out richer and more complex than has usually been supposed.

Shakespeare's Historical Cycle: Organism or Compilation?

IN my *Shakespeare's History Plays*[1] I disagreed with Professor R. A. Law in seeing the two parts of *Henry IV* as closely tied together, variants of a single theme. In a recent article[2] he casts courteous doubt on one of my main positions: that Shakespeare composed his eight plays on English history from Richard II to Bosworth on a single grand conception. Instead, Law pictures Shakespeare feeling his way tentatively from play to play and composing each with reference not to any preconceived plan or set of ideas but to the immediate needs of the present hour. He spends most of his article in pointing to the links between a play and its successor; and he interprets those links in a very limiting sense: they are not parts of a larger concatenation but a mere transition from one otherwise independent unit to another. Further, these links are mainly Shakespeare's own invention, having no source in the chronicles.

In many places Law and I genuinely differ. In others we may differ less than he seems to think, as may appear if I make some points of my position clearer.

When I call Shakespeare's eight connected history plays epic, with England (or Morality-wise Respublica) for hero, I do not mean that before writing he decided to write eight plays, no more and no less, with settled characters. What I do mean is that Shakespeare had steadily in mind certain conceptions of history in general and of the stretch of English history he was concerned with, and that to them he referred, in constantly differing degrees of looseness or closeness, the very varied content of the separate plays. He may have begun writing with no idea of how many plays he meant to run to, and the actual neat arrangement into two balancing

[1] London, 1944, pp. 147-61, 234-44, 298-304.
[2] "Links between Shakespeare's History Plays" in *Studies in Philology*, L (1953), 168-87.

tetralogies may be fortuitous. Or he may have planned exactly eight plays, as Hall divided his history into eight patterned divisions. There is no evidence either way. What matters is that in the plays as we have them there are dominant themes that bind them together and a solemn sense of fateful and divine significance. But this sense does not mean that in writing the separate plays Shakespeare failed in his duty as a playwright. He had to make each play succeed as a unit, as something intelligible to those of the audience who were not familiar with its predecessor. But if during composition such success was in the front of his mind, this does not mean that the larger general conception was not there as a constantly operant background; for it is surely the very nature of Shakespeare's genius to be able to unite the near and the far. And when Shakespeare links one play with another he may do so for the sake both of the immediate sequence and of a great overriding impression. I will illustrate what I mean by speaking of two disputed matters Law treats of: the link between *1* and *2 Henry VI* and the continuity or discontinuity of *1* and *2 Henry IV*.

Law admits that *2* and *3 Henry VI* are linked with exceptional closeness and that they may have been conceived simultaneously. But he does not allow the equal closeness with which the first and second parts are linked to be a parallel, for he adopts the widely accepted notion that the Margaret-Suffolk scenes that end *1 Henry VI* were an afterthought, added in order to connect with *2 Henry VI*, a play earlier in composition but later in the time setting of its subject-matter. Various pieces of external evidence have been adduced to support this order of composition, and these I ignore for the moment. What I do now is to ask the reader to dwell on the likeness between the transitions from the first to the second part and from the second to the third part of *Henry VI*. Law like others says that it was natural and logical that *1 Henry VI* should have ended with the agreement between France and England in V, 4. But he does not say that it was unnatural for the second part to end not with a decisive battle but with the escape of the King, an escape that is caught up in the first words of the third part. The

Margaret-Suffolk episode at the end of the first part is caught up at the beginning of the second part in precisely the same way. Either both transitions are natural and logical or they are both suspect. If there was tampering with the end of the first part, so should there be with the second. But is it necessary to assume any such thing?

Hereward Price, in a booklet too little known in Britain,[1] set forth in detail and very convincingly the close construction of *1 Henry VI*. Of the last act he wrote:

> In Act V the threads of the French war are knotted. Ironically, the English unite when it is too late. They capture and execute Joan, but are obliged to conclude a rotten peace with France. Then Shakespeare introduces new disloyalty. Suffolk woos Margaret, ostensibly to be Henry's wife, really for himself. He buys her by abandoning Anjou and Maine to her father, an inveterate enemy of England . . . and cajoles Henry VI into breaking off an engagement to a princess that would have brought him land, wealth, and influence in France. Thus Act V concludes with frivolous abandonment of English territories, disloyalty at court, weak and imbecile leadership, dishonorable breach of the pledged word.

Thus, Suffolk's wooing of Margaret for his own base ends is a part of the prevailing theme of the play. But Price notes that it also looks forward:

> We must not forget that as *1 Henry VI* is the first part of a tetralogy, Shakespeare left the end hanging in the air. In order to attract people to *2 Henry VI* he deliberately split the marriage of Henry between the two plays.

Further, those who look on the Margaret-Suffolk scenes in the first part as an addition ignore some of the things that their hypothesis entails. Suffolk first appears in the scene in the Temple garden. He is there made out an unscupulous character, an obvious prelude to his unscrupulous behaviour over the King's marriage. But he is also essential in this scene as a principal participant in the original quarrel between

---

[1] *Construction in Shakespeare* (University of Michigan Press, 1951), 24-37.

York and Lancaster. If the Margaret-Suffolk scenes were an addition, then there must have been tampering with the scene in the Temple garden too, and that is a desperate hypothesis, for this scene is a very convincing whole. Moreover it leads straight on to the next scene, between Mortimer and York, ending in Mortimer's death. Once you begin undermining a part of this structure, it is difficult to know where to stop; as difficult as when you begin parcelling out bits of these plays to other dramatists. For myself I find it more difficult to detach the Suffolk-Margaret scenes from *1 Henry VI* than to be sceptical of the external evidence that is supposed to prove this play later than the other two parts. The entry in Henslowe's diary for 3 March 1591-2 recording the play of Henry VI as new and Nashe's reference to Talbot admit of different interpretations and must not be mistaken for narrowly defined evidence. In the present discussions we must not forget that we are in the province not of certainties but of larger or smaller probabilities or improbabilities. It is because I think they have an instinct for the larger probabilities that I support the recent conjectures of Price and Leo Kirschbaum[1] concerning *1 Henry VI*.

But even if the Margaret-Suffolk scenes were an integral part of the play to which they belong they need not on that account be more than an *ad hoc* link to the next play in the series. And I must point out why I do in fact think that they are more. The ideas that underlie and animate Shakespeare's History Plays are simple, the political commonplaces that were accepted by the more thoughtful section of the population. They included the need for a strong, just, and clever king, for the maintenance of the political heirarchies in the state, for the loyalty and altruism of public servants, and above all for the need of harmony in the working of the commonwealth. Along with these general ideas went the special belief in England's being a favoured nation and in a corresponding degradation of the continental nations that were England's chief rivals. By the nature of his material in the stretch of history Shakespeare had fixed on for his

[1] "The Authorship of *1 Henry VI*," *PLMA*, LXVII (1952), 809-22.

theme, France was the country that had to figure through its corruption as a foil to the potential virtue of England. *1 Henry VI* contains all these themes, and the Margaret-Suffolk scenes set them forth with uncommon clarity. At his first appearance Suffolk declares himself bent on his own selfish ends, he will frame the law unto his own will; and his behaviour towards Margaret fits his declaration. He has not the least concern for the good of his country or for the happiness and credit of his King and he woos Margaret for the King in the hope of enjoying her himself. Apart from Margaret he is yet another (and one of the best differentiated) of the ambitious nobles whose portraits give such life, and whose acts such motion, to the *Henry VI* plays. As such he is from his first entry thoroughly integrated into the pattern of the play. Margaret has the function of continuing the theme of French perversion after the removal of La Pucelle. She is unlike La Pucelle in being no witch, but she is bold and bad, the she-wolf of France owning a French ferocity of which the massacre of St Bartholomew was the great modern example. Like Suffolk she is from her first entrance thoroughly integrated into the pattern of the play. I find it hard to believe that the total shares of these two characters in the whole tetralogy were not generally roughed out before Shakespeare began composition. But of course this does not mean that he was not free to have second thoughts and to modify as he went along.

I conclude therefore that the end of *1 Henry VI* has both a general and a special purpose. It reinforces the total theme of the whole tetralogy and it prepares the way for the next item in the sequence.

Coming to *Henry IV* I should like to refer not only to R. A. Law's article but to M. A. Shaaber's persuasive plea for a complete break between the first and second parts.[1] First, Law attributes to me a definiteness I do not aspire to, when he says that I support Dover Wilson's notion of absolute continuity including the performance of both parts on successive days. What I meant was that I agreed with

---

[1] *Joseph Quincy Adams Memorial Studies* (Washington, 1948), pp. 217-27.

Dover Wilson in seeing a similarity of conception in the two plays that was accounted for most simply by a general, preconceived, plan. And that is different from holding that Shakespeare had settled all the details of the second part before beginning to write the first. On the contrary I think it probable that the success of Falstaff in the first part influenced the share Falstaff had in the second. Shaaber is thoroughly fair to his opponents when he admits that the Prince's reform and the rejection of Falstaff were so much a part of English historical mythology that Shakespeare must have intended to include them in his historical cycle from the start; and his contention that these were intended originally for the opening of *Henry V* is possible and indeed cannot be disproved. Once more we are in the region of competing probabilities, and I find the following hypothesis more probable. Shakespeare planned his *Henry IV* on the scheme of two parts similar in that each shows the hero tested, dissimilar in that the tests are different. The first part shows the Prince tested in the chivalric virtues, the second shows him tested in the civil. The rejection of Falstaff in favour of the Chief Justice is the culmination to the second test.

Shaaber has an excellent last paragraph on Shakespeare's method of working, one can say his opportunism. With it I heartily agree. But what I want to insist on is that opportunism does not exclude the larger plan. Shakespeare could plan massively, but he was not a slave to his plan. He was always ready to modify it in the interests of the immediate dramatic success. To apply this principle to the two parts of *Henry IV*: Shakespeare planned them generally from a distance but he allowed the success of the first to influence the execution of the second. It is the same principle I have argued for at the end of *1 Henry VI*: the combination of the near and the far, of the short-term and the long-term policy.

To revert to the *Henry VI* plays, it is a melancholy business participating in the disputes about them, for there is no possibility of compromise or respect for the other side's opinion. Either you or your opponent is crashingly wrong: the vision of Shakespeare thou dost see is my vision's greatest enemy. I am now thinking not of the more restricted matters at issue between Professor Law and myself but of the large question of authorship. When in the *Composition of Shakespeare's Plays*[1] the late Albert Feuillerat says that in the *Contention* there is not a line that can be attributed to Shakespeare, I can only gasp and point, for instance, to these lines:

> Then will I raise aloft the milke-white Rose,
> With whose sweete smell the aire shall be perfumed,
> And in my Standard beare the Armes of *Yorke*,
> To grapple with the House of *Lancaster*:
> And force perforce, ile make him yeeld the Crowne,
> Whose bookish rule hath puld faire England Downe.

or

> Here could I breath my soule into the aire,
> As milde and gentle as the new borne babe,
> That dies with mother dugge betweene his lips.

If he can't attribute these lines to Shakespeare, well I can; and no rational argument can follow on these crude assertions. The available facts (apart from aesthetic considerations), however informative on theatrical conditions, do not settle the disputed matter of authorship and admit of the most discrepant interpretations. Thus the opposed parties have really no option but to turn back to back at the very outset and proceed to construct their own edifices knowing that either theirs or their opponents' is falsely based, vitiated from the start. It is not a pleasant piece of knowledge, and incidentally it takes the zest out of the game of heaving an odd brick at your opponent, for what is the use of scoring a minor point if you are wrong throughout?

If the dispute went no further than the scholars, no great harm would ensue. But it has certainly served to keep *Henry VI* from the usual repertory of acted plays. All the more credit to the very few who have actually produced them. The latest production is by the Birmingham Repertory Company, now running at the Old Vic in London. This production greatly confirmed my opinion that Shake-

[1] New Haven, 1953, p. 99.

speare was the author and that he constructed massively and with thought. But then I brought my opinion with me ready made. Could the ghost of Albert Feuillerat have been there it would doutbless have had the very opposite opinion confirmed.

Why did Shakespeare write "Henry VIII"?

THERE is a great deal to connect *Henry VIII* with the age in which it was written. For instance, the play's latest editor[1] may be right in thinking that it was elicited to grace the rejoicings over the wedding of Princess Elizabeth and the Elector Palatine even though it is absent from the Chamber Accounts' list of the plays performed on the occasion. Again, while I cannot agree with Frank Kermode[2] in his plea that the play is mainly in the "falls" tradition established and popularised by the *Mirror for Magistrates* (a plea he makes at the cost of turning Cranmer into a virtual fourth victim after Buckingham, Katherine, and Wolsey), I can agree that there may be some connection between the way Shakespeare treats the falls of the first three and the change from the heroic to the pathetic that took place in the "fall" literature of the Jacobean age. And again, if Shakespeare wrote the whole of the play he showed that he was alive to certain trends in contemporary versification.

Nevertheless, I cannot think that any contemporary incitement constituted the sole or the chief cause of Shakespeare's undertaking this last commitment. The tone of the play does not suggest (as *Lycidas* or the *Wreck of the Deutschland* suggests) that the poet had been brimming with new matter eagerly awaiting an invitation to be released: that, for instance, he was fired by a contemporary political concern to seek expression in a portion of history he had not yet touched; still less that he was anxious to reanimate the *Mirror* tradition; and again still less that he wanted to conduct a prosodical experiment. The play of *Henry VIII* has been generally underprized till the last few years, but it is vain to pretend that it shows the consistent vitality one

---

[1] R. A. Foakes in the revised Arden series, 1957.
[2] F. Kermode in *Durham University Journal*, March 1948, p. 51.

would expect from a truly new creation. It is constructed with care and skill; it rises fitfully to great animation; but for sustained energy it cannot compare with either the *Winter's Tale* or the *Tempest*. Any plausible conjecture concerning the puzzle of why Shakespeare wrote the play at all as against that of why he treated this or that episode as he did, is not likely to derive from reflecting on contemporary conditions. Ask a tired and ageing author for something new, and he will first consider what still remains of his reduced stock: can the depleted larder after all furnish another meal? If on looking round he finds that there are some remnants he would like to make use of, he may well say *yes*, even after initial reluctance. And so I ask, what was Shakespeare likely to have in store towards the end of his life relating to the age of Henry VIII?

Although proof is impossible, I am convinced that in his early years Shakespeare had read and digested Hall's *Chronicle* with much seriousness and enthusiasm, that he derived his philosophy of history from Hall chiefly, and that he dreamt of dramatising the main events recorded by him. That Hall's *Chronicle* set out to culminate in the reign of Henry VIII is evident from the title page and that it indeed did so is evident from Hall's devoting nearly half his book to that reign. The expanded title of Hall's *Chronicle* is as follows:

> The union of the two noble and illustre families of Lancaster and York, being long in continual dissension for the crown of this noble realm, with all the acts done in both the time of the princes, both of the one lineage and of the other, beginning at the time of King Henry the Fourth, the first author of this division, and successively proceeding to the reign of the high and prudent prince Henry the Eighth, the indubitable flower and very heir of the said lineages.

If Shakespeare pondered Hall so earnestly and if Hall makes so much of the reign of Henry VIII, it is most unlikely that Shakespeare did not at some time intend to include that reign in his dramatic scope. It is also worth checking this likelihood by recalling the way Henry presented himself to the Elizabethans. This way Hardin Craig has described as follows:

> Modern readers are often surprised to see how well the Eliza-
> bethans thought of King Henry VIII. They regarded him as a
> favourer of learning and a champion of his country against the
> greed and oppression of Rome. He was the fairy King Oberon to
> Spenser and perhaps to Shakespeare. He was bluff King Hal, a
> popular sovereign and one whose heart was tender towards his
> subjects. The Elizabethans actually knew far less about him than
> we do, were less offended by his autocracy, and were more willing
> than we to condone his immoralities.[1]

The moment when we should expect Shakespeare to have
gone on to the reign of Henry VIII was of course after
having finished *Richard III*. And the last words of that play,
though spoken by Richmond, emerge from their strictly
dramatic context into general patriotic sentiments which are
those of dramatist and audience at once and are not unlikely
to reveal how Shakespeare meant to treat English history
after Bosworth. The words centre on the "union of the two
noble and illustre families of Lancaster and York."

> O now let Richmond and Elizabeth,
> The true succeeders of each royal house,
> By God's fair ordinance conjoin together!
> And let their heirs, God, if thy will be so,
> Enrich the time to come with smooth-faced peace,
> With smiling plenty and fair prosperous days!

Unfortunately these lines are ambiguous, equally apt as an
epilogue to early happenings or as an announcement of
future plans, and give no clue to Shakespeare's intentions;
but at least they make it clear that at that moment he had the
happenings recounted in the second half of Hall's *Chronicle*
very much in mind.

Why, when he turned to history once again, Shakespeare
went back in time instead of forward we can only guess. It
may be that he was impelled to compete with Daniel's *Civil*

---

[1] *An Interpretation of Shakespeare* (New York, 1948), p. 363.

Wars; it may be that he could not bear to leave youthful and immature versions of the reigns of Henry IV and Henry V unrevised. But a quite sufficient reason can be found in the nature of the material provided by the reigns of Henry VII and Henry VIII.

Although Ford was to make a creditable play out of Perkin Warbeck's rebellion, this even was not crucial in English history, being but a mutter of a passed storm not a present and dangerous storm in its own right. Nor was there anything in the reign of Henry VII to compare in dramatic power with the events that led up to it. Even what Hall called the "triumphant reign of Henry the Eighth" was in its central parts poor in drama. For all his knightly and intellectual equipment Henry never achieved anything heroic. He never led his subjects to an Agincourt; and, if the Reformation reached England in his reign, there was nothing heroic in his share in the process. As bluff King Hal and a popular monarch he was suited to be the hero of a hearty comedy but not of a solemn and eventful patriotic play, of the kind Shakespeare was committed to. As the "indubitable flower and very heir of the lineages of Lancaster and York" and as the father of Elizabeth he had an impressive static significance but he could not exert a strong attraction for a dramatist longing to present stirring and significant action. As a principal figure he was better suited to a pageant than to a play. Of far greater dramatic interest were the men and women who prospered and whom Henry proceeded to humble; and the chief of these was Wolsey, whose fall had been the subject of one of the tragedies in *A Mirror for Magistrates*.

That between the dates of his two historical tetralogies Shakespeare had stored his mind with thoughts about a possible play or plays on the reign of Henry VIII I am convinced; that those thoughts corresponded to some degree with what he was destined to write many years later I consider highly probable. Nevertheless, the possibilities he then saw were not attractive enough to make him continue history after the Battle of Bosworth, and he preferred to turn to earlier events. Loyalty to Hall would still impel him to glorify the Tudors or at least England under the Tudors; and it is likely that in *King John*, the Protestantism, the figure of the Bastard Falconbridge and his words on England point veiledly to such a glorification. But Shakespeare may well have felt that he had failed to do his complete duty in this matter; and the feeling may have remained, slightly nagging, in his mind. In sum, the fruit of his reflections on the reign of Henry VIII was put in cold storage in his mental repository, with a kind of conscience that some day he ought to pull it out.

Though I think it likely that Shakespeare had reflected in his earlier years on the dramatic possibilities of the reign of Henry VIII I refrain from conjecturing whether or not he had gone farther and made plans or even begun to put these plans in hand. He may easily have intended more than one play: for instance one in the *Mirror* mode and one in as near the mode of *Henry V* as the material would allow, glorifying his country. But anyhow such conjectures are irrelevant, as being subservient to the greater probability that, when Shakespeare in his last years was asked for a play suitable for royal rejoicing or resolved on his own account to fulfil an old obligation, his mind was stored with certain dramatic material derived from events in the reign of Henry VIII. Even if he had once intended more than one play on it, he now lacked the energy to fulfil such an intention; and his problem was to devise something that would combine the interest of the different "falls" with his obligation to glorify the Tudors.

Opinion has differed on how far Shakespeare succeeded in the task he set himself. On the whole his success has been under-estimated; and, though I cannot follow him in his pleas for a superlative quality of the whole play and its profound symbolic meanings, we are indebted to Wilson Knight[1] for having argued so vehemently that the play presents an interlocked whole. For myself, I find *Henry VIII* very much the play you would expect from Shakespeare at this time in his career. Confronted with a very heterogeneous

[1] In *The Crown of Life*, London, 1947.

material—a total material he might not have chosen, given a clean slate—he uses his prodigious skill and experience as a dramatic technician to make the best of it. Beginning with a scene, the account of the Field of the Cloth of Gold, capable of pointing two ways, to the glory of royal pomp and to its transience, he follows the second way and develops the themes of great men's falls. But not without interruption, for he makes Wolsey during the course of his own self-destruction provide through the entertainment he offers Henry (I, iv) not only one of the main reasons for that destruction, the meeting of Henry and Anne Bullen, but the introduction of the second, patriotic, master-theme of the play. Contrariwise, near the end, the trial of Cranmer at once prolongs the "fall" theme into the context of the glorification of England and through its happy ending, assured by the now better developed judgement of Henry, is itself a part of that glorification. Such examples of close construction are but two among many others, most of which have by now been noticed by the critics. All these, taken together, should command our high admiration. Nevertheless, they belong to the intellect more than to the imagination, being constructed, I believe, according to a prearranged pattern and not growing out of the requirements of the evolving play.

Exactly as we should expect in an ageing man, although the old vitality breaks out in places into highly dramatic broken rhythms and strikingly new metaphors, competence, pleasing because of its great skill, in the main prevails. Take this ending of I, iv, where Henry speaks of Anne Bullen:

King   By heaven, she is a dainty one. Sweet heart,
        I were unmannerly to take you out
        And not to kiss you. A health, gentlemen!
        Let it go round.
Wol.   Sir Thomas Lovell, is the banquet ready
        I' the privy chamber?
Lov.   Yes, my lord.
Wol.   Your grace,
        I fear, with dancing is a little heated.

King   I fear, too much.
Wol.   There's fresher air, my lord,
       In the next chamber.
King   Lead in your ladies every one. Sweet partner,
       I must not yet forsake you. Let's be merry,
       Good my lord cardinal: I have half a dozen healths
       To drink to these fair ladies and a measure
       To lead 'em once again; and then let's dream
       Who's best in favour. Let the music knock it.

These lines end a scene once usually attributed to Fletcher.
I can see no strong reason for attributing them to him. On
the other hand, in their perfection and in their mediocrity
they are exactly what you would expect of the Master in his
old age, the product of a perfected technique yet so little
animated by his individual fire as to approximate to the
current norm of the time.

My conjecture, then, is that Shakespeare had had the
material for *Henry VIII* in his mind for a long time; that
either because he was asked for a play or because his conscience pricked him he decided to dramatise that material;
that he showed the greatest technical skill in carrying out a
difficult piece of work; but that the work as completed lacks
the creative energy that animates his greatest plays.

Finally, let me point to the puzzle of the prologue. Of the
critics I have read, only Wilson Knight comments on the
discrepancy between prologue and play; and he does not go
far enough, merely remarking that it "scarcely covers the
whole action." In truth, it asserts with the utmost emphasis,
repeating the original assertion at the end, that the play will
be about the fall of great men from high estate, and gives the
undoubted impression that it will concern nothing else; thus
ignoring about half the play. And not only that, but in the
middle it goes out of its way to tell a plain untruth: that there
will be no bawdy; a statement all the more surprising because
as well as later there is plenty of amiable bawdy in the scene
between Anne Bullen and the old lady (II, iii), which occurs
within the main body of the "fall" material. I mention these
things because they have not, to my knowledge, been

mentioned before. But why the writer of the prologue (and I cannot see that anyone has a better right to it than Shakespeare) should have told wanton lies I cannot begin to perceive. Anyhow I have made conjectures enough already; and further conjectures on the prologue I leave to others.

Reality and Fantasy in Elizabethan Literature

MOST people will admit the elements of both reality and fantasy in the Elizabethan Age. The men of it were anything but impractical and dreamers. They were full of earthly enterprise; they took risks but they calculated them; they made daring voyages but not without profit; they achieved a practical compromise in matters of religion. On the other hand, when it came to self-expression either in dress or in speech, they liked to be fantastic. Consider the sheer elaboration of detail in the dresses of Queen Elizabeth as shown in the portraits; consider the stylistic writhings of the average address of publisher or author to his readers. This, for instance, is how the printer of the first quarto of *Troilus and Cressida* began his address to the reader:

> *A never writer to an ever reader. News.* Eternal reader, you have here a new play, never staled with the stage, never clapper-clawed with the palms of the vulgar, and yet passing full of the palm comical; for it is a birth of your brain that never undertook anything comical vainly: and were but the vain names of comedies changed for the titles of commodities, or of plays for pleas, you should see all those grand censors that now style them such vanities flock to them for the main grace of their gravities.

And so on and so on, to more and more vile puns and other obfuscations of plain sense.

Well, it is easy to recognise these two qualities, reality and fantasy; it is far more difficult to think of them together, to fuse them. But it is precisely this fusion that gives the Elizabethan age its special character. One of the people who understood this truth was Charles Lamb. This comes out in his defence of Sidney against the attacks of Hazlitt, who thought that the extravagances of Sidney's style betokened an otiose, perverse, and unnecessary inflation. Lamb saw that, on the contrary, they were organic:

55

The images which lie before our feet (though by some accounted the only natural) are the least natural for the high Sydnean love to express its fancies by.

Lamb also saw that the Elizabethan drama, for all its fantastic and improbable happenings, was firmly grounded in morality; and it is this moral basis which Lamb in his *Characters of Dramatic Writers Contemporary with Shakespeare* —that annotated anthology of Elizabethan and Jacobean drama which had so much to do in restoring it to public favour—sought to illustrate. He said in his preface:

When I selected for publication, in 1808, specimens of the English Dramatic Poets who lived about the time of Shakespeare, the kind of extracts which I was anxious to give were, not so much passages of wit and humour, though the old plays are rich in such, as scenes of passion, sometimes of the deepest quality, interesting situations, serious descriptions, that which is more nearly allied to poetry than to wit, and to tragic rather than to comic poetry. The plays which I made choice of were, with few exceptions, such as treat of human life and manners, rather than masques and Arcadian pastorals, with their train of abstractions, unimpassioned deities, passionate mortals—Claius, and Medorus, and Amintas, and Amaryllis. My leading design was, to illustrate what can be called the moral sense of our ancestors.

Turn now from the critics to the Elizabethan writers themselves. People recognise the importance of Hooker in the history of the English Church, of his refusal to yield either to the Catholics on the one side or to the Puritans on the other. They look on him as one of the great, practical, stabilising influences of Anglicanism. People also recognise the charm of Marlowe's extravagances in *Tamburlaine*, as in this passage when the conqueror claims that legions of spirits fight on his side and that the Goddess of Victory herself alights upon his tent:

Our conquering swords shall marshall us the way
We use to march upon the slaughtered foe,
Trampling their bowels with our horses' hoofs;

Brave horses, bred on the white Tartarian hills.
My camp is like to Julius Caesar's host,
That never fought but had the victory.
Legions of spirits fleeting in the air
Direct our bullets and our weapons points;
And when she sees our bloody colours spread,
Then Victory begins to take her flight,
Resting herself upon my milk-white tent.

But how many of us think of Hooker and Marlowe together?
How many consider that the great picture of Order (what
Hooker calls Law in general) that is built up in the *Laws of
Ecclesiastical Polity* should be thought of as, among other
things, the splendid and solemn background before which
the feats and blasphemies of Tamburlaine are presented. The
very legions of spirits that Tamburlaine claimed to direct his
bullets would lose most of their point without the contemporary belief in angels, devils, and other spirits "betwixt
angelical and human kind." To keep Hooker and Marlowe
apart is an error much like the still common assumption that
the audience of a great preacher and the spectators of a bear-
fight were a different body of men. True, some of the more
puritanical of the audience would have avoided the bear-
fight, and some of the more dissolute spectators have avoided
the sermon; but a big middle block was common to both
activities.

Or take Walter Raleigh. We tend to cut him in two; to
think of him first as the courtier and the explorer, and then
either to ignore or to keep apart the other Raleigh, historian
of the world, whose introductory chapter is as solemn and
pious and cosmic as Hooker. But Raleigh had always been a
theologian. Early in his life, at a certain dinner-party, he is
recorded to have talked theology: unorthodox, it is true, and
designed to shock a divine then present; but sufficient to
show that his interests already lay in that direction.

Even in their conception of the cosmos the Elizabethans
combined the rigid and the fanciful. Theologically they were
uncompromisingly Protestant and accepted the Pauline
theology of creation, fall through sin, vicarious atonement

and redemption, and the various stages of justification, sanctification, glorification; at the same time they retained portions of the old, complicated cosmogony of the Middle Ages. They were serious enough about the outlines of the scheme, about the general order of creation: God, the angels, man, the beasts, and inanimate nature, the stars, and the elements. But over the details they were far less serious; and all sorts of fanciful options were open to them. Take the matter of angels and devils. In the Middle Ages it really mattered that the angels should be divided into nine—no more and no less—orders according to the account, accepted as orthodox, of Dionysius the Areopagite, a Christian neo-platonist of the fifth century A.D. It was also important that these nine orders of angels should be balanced by nine orders of devils. These accurate balances mattered to the mathematically minded folk of the Middle Ages. There is plenty of writing about angels and devils in the Elizabethan age, but the old insistence on precision has gone and we find ourselves in a realm at once imprecise and fanciful. You need not go farther than Burton for an example of this fantasy. But remember that it co-existed with the rigidity of the Protestant scheme and the firm outlines of the Elizabethan picture of world organisation.

I turn now to some concrete, literary examples of these contrasts the fusion of which gives Elizabethan literature its proper character.

It is admitted that the Pastoral is a common literary form in Elizabethan days; and yet it is often assumed that this mode is a sideline, a piece of agreeable but isolated fantasy. True, a play like Fletcher's *Faithful Shepherdess* is pure pastoral diversion. But turn to a greater, and a centrally Elizabethan figure, Spenser, and you will see how reality and fantasy can be equally present in the same poem, and how the poem's point and delight is the fusion of these apparently incongruous elements. The poem I have in mind is *Colin Clout's Come Home Again*. It was written just about when Shakespeare was beginning to succeed as a dramatist, and since it was by the foremost poet of the age, Spenser, he is certain to have known it. Here are some of its circumstances.

In 1589 Raleigh and Spenser met in Ireland. Raleigh had come over to look after his estates; Spenser had been a civil servant there for some years and had now settled as a country gentleman. He had written the first three books of the *Faerie Queene*. The two men of letters met and read their verses to each other. Raleigh, then in high favour at court, persuaded Spenser to return with him and try his luck with his new poem. In October 1589 they arrived. Spenser proceeded to publish his books of the *Faerie Queene*, trumpeted by a series of eulogies by contemporary authors and prefaced by a letter addressed to Raleigh. Poetically Spenser scored a great success: personally he achieved little; for his enemy Burleigh probably barred his way to advancement. Granted a pension of £50 a year, he had no option but to return to his Irish estate. Most of these actual happenings are described in the poem.

When you come to the execution, what a change! To narrate these true events Spenser chose the remote and fantastic form of the pastoral. Moreover some of the events were the least suited to pastoral treatment, because they had to do with the sea. An actual sea voyage had to be described. The Queen is introduced; and she, so soon after the defeat of the Armada, must be complimented as mistress of the waves. Raleigh, though an Irish landowner, could hardly be mentioned without some maritime reference. Now, except for an occasional dip of his respective kind, neither sheep nor shepherd has much acquaintance with water. In fact a marine subject is perfectly unsuited to the Pastoral. Does this unsuitability deter Spenser? Not a bit, for it gives him the chance of the greater ingenuity of fantasy. Elizabeth, or Cynthia as he calls her, the moon-goddess who ruled the tides, is a shepherdess, the supreme shepherdess, but she rules the Ocean. Its waves are her pastures; its fish and monsters are her herds. Raleigh becomes one of the under-shepherds who along with Triton and Proteus drives the herds of what Spenser calls "the stinking seales and porcpisces" to pasture. The passage deserves generous quotation, partly for its inherent beauty and partly for its containing a line on which Wordsworth in a famous sonnet committed one of his happiest poetical larcenies. The setting is the voyage across the Irish Channel.

> Then hartelesse quite, and full of inward feare,
> That shepheard I besought to me to tell,
> Under what skie, or in what world we were,
> In which I saw no living people dwell.
> Who, me recomforting all that he might,
> Told me that that same was the Regiment
> Of a great shepheardesse, that Cynthia hight,
> His liege, his Ladie, and his lifes Regent.
> If then (quoth I) a shepheardesse she bee,
> Where be the flockes and heards, which she doth keep?
> And where may I the hills and pastures see,
> On which she useth for to feed her sheepe?
> These be the hills, (quoth he,) the surges hie,
> On which faire Cynthia her heards doth feed:
> Her heards be thousand fishes with their frie,
> Which in the bosome of the billowes breed.
> Of them the shepheard which hath charge in chief,
> Is Triton, blowing loud his wreathed horne:
> At sound whereof, they all for their relief
> Wend too and fro at evening and at morne.
> And Proteus eke with him does drive his heard
> Of stinking seales and porcpisces together,
> With hoary head and deawy dropping beard,
> Compelling them which way he list, and whether.
> And I, among the rest, of many least,
> Have in the Ocean charge to me assignd;
> Where I will live or die at her beheast,
> And serve and honour her with faithful mind.

There indeed is fantasy. As to the realism, Spenser has bitter things to say of court-life, its vanities and ingratitude, but I choose rather for illustration a passage describing the actual journey from Ireland to England. In a way it is as fantastically remote from realism as what I have just read. The travellers, instead of booking a passage and regarding the time and being occupied with getting luggage aboard, "wander" quite aimlessly to the shore, Colin (or Spenser)

having nothing with him but his oaten quill; and then as if
from nowhere a vessel appears and takes them up. But the
real terrors of the sea (when even a channel crossing was an
adventure) and the glamour of the ship (when ships were ships
and not floating hotels) are described with a sincerity that
shows how little Spenser found the pastoral form a hindrance.

> So to the sea we came; the sea, that is
> A world of waters heaped up on hie,
> Rolling like mountaines in wide wildernesse,
> Horrible, hideous, roaring with hoarse crie.
>   And is the sea (quoth Coridon) so fearfull?
>   Fearful much more (quoth he) then hart can fear:
> Thousand wyld beasts with deep mouthes gaping direfull
> Therein stil wait poore passengers to teare.
> Who life doth loath, and longs death to behold,
> Before he die, alreadie dead with feare,
> And yet would live with heart halfe stonie cold,
> Let him to sea, and he shall see it there.
> And yet as ghastly dreadfull, as it seemes,
> Bold men, presuming life for gaine to sell,
> Dare tempt that gulf, and in those wandring stremes
> Seek waies unknowne, waies leading down to hell.
> For, as we stood there waiting on the strond,
> Behold, an huge great vessell to us came,
> Dauncing upon the waters back to lond,
> As if it scornd the daunger of the same;
> Yet was it but a wooden frame and fraile,
> Glewed togither with some subtile matter.
> Yet had it armes and wings, and head and taile,
> And life to move it selfe upon the water.
> Strange thing! how bold and swift the monster was,
> That neither car'd for wynd, nor haile, nor raine,
> Nor swelling waves, but thorough them did passe
> So proudly, that she made them roare againe.

It is a dazzling description of a real sailing-ship riding the
waves; and it illustrates my assertion about the age of Elizabeth.
It is, for all the fantasy, astonishingly simple. We all get our
picture of that ship quite clearly; we know just where we are.

I hope the passages I have read will dissipate any notion that the Pastoral is necessarily a minor, non-serious literary form and will have brought home to you the range of the great Elizabethans.

Or take an author of a very different temperament from the "sage and serious" Spenser, that versatile "University Wit," Nashe: playwright, pamphleteer, novelist. Stylistically, he is the perfect example of Elizabethan froth, fancy, and high spirits. And yet behind all these is the solemn reality of the accepted world-organisation. His *Pierce Penniless, his Supplication to the Devil* is a lively satirical pamphlet best known for its defence of poetry and its early reference to a historical play about Talbot (probably Shakespeare's first part of *Henry VI*). But it is carefully constructed on the medieval pattern of the Seven Deadly Sins. Or take his *Summer's Last Will and Testament*, a highly artificial play about the seasons, mingling the different modes of the Masque, the Pastoral, and the Morality. Here again there is the assurance that the solemn reality of the accepted world-organisation is behind these modes. Spring is a young, riotous character and refuses to be confined to bounds; it is in his nature to wanton and spread himself; and this is his self-justification:

> The world is transitory; it was made of nothing, and it must to nothing: wherefore, if we will do the will of our high Creator (whose will it is that it pass to nothing) we must help to consume it to nothing.

Solstice, keeping the proportions fixed between night and day, is a different character. He is equated with the balance of justice in the state and he illustrates one of those great correspondences between the different orders of the universe that form so important a part of the Elizabethan myth of world organisation: the correspondence between the physical world and the body politic.

Summer	What dost thou with those balances thou bearest?
Solstice	In them I weigh the day and night alike:
	The white glass is the hour-glass of the day,
	The black one the just measure of the night.

> One more than other holdeth not a grain;
> Both serve time's just proportion to maintain.
>
> *Summer*   I like thy moderation wondrous well;
> And this thy balance weighing the white glass
> And black with equal poise and steady hand
> A pattern is to princes and great men
> How to weigh all estates indifferently;
> The spiritualty and temporalty alike:
> Neither to be too prodigal of smiles,
> Nor too severe with smiling without cause.

It is only a detail but it implies the whole elaborate scheme in the background.

At the end of the same play Nashe gives us the same contrast that Spenser gave in *Colin Clout*, that between fantasy and acute actuality. The play itself has been predominantly airy and gay, when suddenly Nashe gives us the bitter reality of the moment. It is known that, on account of the plague, Michaelmas Term of the Inns of Court in 1593 was held not in London but in St Albans; and Nashe's lyric refers to the event. Summer has died, and Winter with all its woes approaches:

> Autumn hath all the summer's fruitful treasure;
> Gone is our sport, fled is poor Croydon's pleasure.
> Short days, sharp days, long nights come on apace.
> Ah, who can hide us from the winter's face?
> Cold doth increase, the sickness will not cease;
> And here we lie, God knows, with little ease.
>   From winter, plague, and pestilence, good Lord, deliver us!
>
> London doth mourn, Lambeth is quite forlorn;
> Trades cry, woe worth that ever they were born.
> The want of term is town and city's harm.
> Close chambers do we want to keep us warm.
> Long banished must we live from our friends;
> This low-built house will bring us to our ends.
>   From winter, plague, and pestilence, good Lord, deliver us!

This closeness to the actual event is wonderfully effective in validating the fantasy that has gone before. We are assured that the fantasy is not a sign of weakness but of a pressure of vitality that insists on the ornate to reinforce the simple. Life presents itself not in one way but in all sorts of ways demanding all sorts of styles in their expression.

I come now to Shakespeare and I am embarrassed by the range of possible illustration. What I shall do mainly is to allow the illustrations given already to lead on to those from the master dramatist.

Shakespeare showed the characteristic Elizabethan contrasts from the very first; and, being what he was, in a variety greater than the others could attain. Sometimes the contrast was between fantasy and real life, like what we found in Nashe; sometimes that between conventional or official sentiments and real life; sometimes between conventional and natural behaviour in his characters; sometimes between serious current doctrine and fantastic incident. In Shakespeare's earliest tragedy, *Titus Andronicus*, there is the contrast between the conventional horrors, inherited from Ovid and Seneca and exaggerated by the bursting vitality of a young and growing author, and the genuine and deeply felt political doctrine given in this speech of Marcus Andronicus near the end of the play:

> You sad-fac'd men, people and sons of Rome,
> By uproar sever'd like a flight of fowl
> Scatter'd by winds and high tempestuous gusts,
> O, let me teach you how to knit again
> This scatter'd corn into one mutual sheaf,
> These broken limbs again into one body;
> Lest Rome herself be bane unto herself,
> And she whom mighty kingdoms court'sy to,
> Like a forlorn and desperate castaway,
> Do shameful execution on herself.

By *mutual sheaf* Shakespeare means a sheaf in which every ear, in mutual co-operation, willingly makes up the whole: a phrase implying the grand doctrine of order or degree. I grant that in this play itself the fantasy of blood and the living contemporary doctrine may not fuse; but the two elements are evidently there.

In the earliest History Plays Shakespeare's prevailing tone is that of a conventional heightening suitable to the high political theme. It is a style which at its worst touches melodrama, at its best the true storm of political passions. This is how Humphrey of Gloucester in the second part of *Henry VI*, knowing that his life is threatened by his enemies, describes their characters and motives.

> Beaufort's red sparkling eyes blab his heart's malice,
> And Suffolk's cloudy brow his stormy hate;
> Sharp Buckingham unburthens with his tongue
> The envious load that lies upon his heart;
> And dogged York, that reaches at the moon,
> Whose overweening arm I have pluck'd back,
> By false accuse doth level at my life;
> And you, my sovran lady, with the rest
> Causeless have laid disgraces on my head
> And with your best endeavour have stirr'd up
> My liefest liege to be mine enemy.

Nevertheless, from the very first, Shakespeare crossed this high, official, political writing with touches from nature. In the first part of *Henry VI* Regnier says of the English:

> I think by some odd gimmers or device
> Their arms are set like clocks, still to strike on.

And Talbot, in distress before Orleans, exclaims

> My thoughts are whirled like a potter's wheel.

Here are two homely images, taken from direct, personal observation.

As Shakespeare matured, the different elements of his contrasts are not merely juxtaposed but fused. I mentioned that Nashe brought in his song about the plague to cross the fantasy of his *Summer's Last Will and Testament*. Near the time of this play Shakespeare did just the same kind of thing in *Love's Labour's Lost*. He put at the end of the enchanting confectionery that forms the body of his play the two songs about spring and winter: "When daisies pied and violets blue" and "When icicles hang by the wall." In these he resorted to absolute truth and homeliness: the girls bleaching their summer frocks, the coughing in church in winter, and Tom carrying logs for the fire in the hall. But though this exquisite ending surprises us we are assured somehow that Shakespeare meant it all along. In the body of the play he is never grimly absorbed by the ingenuities of plot and language; he knows exactly how much of himself to give to them; and we feel that he has all sorts of things there in reserve to produce if he finds it fitting. The songs at the end are a part of the store that co-existed all along with the concerns of the moment.

There may still be a danger of thinking that as he grew older Shakespeare relied progressively less on convention and more on nature, as if the less you had of the one and the more you had of the other, the better. In actual fact Shakespeare throughout his maturity always mixed the subtlest truth with the grossest improbabilities, just as we now recognise that his characters can shift, individually, from the most advanced psychological realism to the most impersonal ejaculation of rhetoric. Enobarbus, we now see, ceases temporarily to be Enobarbus when Shakespeare makes him deliver an ecstatic description of Cleopatra in her barge; a description he is the last character in the play by standards of realistic fitness to be likely to utter. The truth in these matters is not that Shakespeare became progressively more natural but that he always worked through fusing the natural and the improbable; it was his method of creating a world of many dimensions.

I spoke of Spenser's marine pastoral, *Colin Clout's Come Home Again*; and I can illustrate Shakespeare's fusion of the natural and the outrageous well enough through his own ventures in the pastoral mode. It used to be the fashion to say that Shakespeare showed his superiority here over his fellows in the reality of his pastoral setting; and to suggest that he learnt his lesson as he went along. *As You Like It* was represented as his experiment: a masterpiece of comedy indeed but still rather "artificial" on the pastoral side. You find there a treatment of the pastoral delightful indeed but sophisticated and lacking that naturalness which *ex hypothesi* the best pastoral should possess. Shakespeare, it seems, was too aware of the absurdities contained in such a pastoral as *Colin Clout* to be able to let himself go and expatiate in his own English countryside. He introduces his genuine rustics, Audrey and William, only to contrast their boorishness with the Arcadian civility of Phoebe and Silvius. Also we know that the Forest of Arden, though providing the core of the play, is an interlude. The court is never assimilated to that wild setting. In other words Shakespeare, we have been told, did not surrender to the pastoral in *As You Like It*. But in his other pastoral, the Bohemian scenes in the *Winter's Tale*, he is said to have achieved this, giving us the true English countryside with his whole heart and without any critical comparison with other more sophisticated modes of existence. And the conception dovetails nicely with Shakespeare's retirement from active theatre management to the rural repose of Stratford-upon-Avon and a return to the pastoral remembrances of his youth.

Up to a point this description of a change between the two plays is true. In the *Winter's Tale* Shakespeare commits himself far more deeply to his pastoral descriptions. The shearing feast is a more genuine pastoral event, more closely allied to a real country happening than anything in *As You Like It*. There is nothing in the earlier play to compare, for instance, with these lines of the old shepherd exhorting Perdita to put more energy into her work of hospitality:

> Fie, daughter! when my old wife liv'd, upon
> This day she was both pantler, butler, cook,
> Both dame and servant; welcom'd all, serv'd all:
> Would sing her song and dance her turn; now here,
> At upper end o' the table, now i'the middle;
> On his shoulder, and his; her face o' fire
> With labour and the thing she took to quench it,
> She would to each one sip.

And who would say that Perdita's famous account of the flowers—daffodils, violets, primroses—fails to recall the real English countryside? But one must not go too far. Remember first that Spenser, for all his fantasy in *Colin Clout*, had described the sea with an immediate sense of its actual existence as strong as Shakespeare's sense of pastoral England. And as to an all-pervading nature in Shakespeare, if you are not careful you soon run into absurdity. Perdita's flower-speech may have elements of nature in it, but what of Perdita herself? Judge by nature, by the laws of probability, and it is outrageous that this girl, still very young and brought up entirely without education and among illiterates, should be perfectly at home with the exalted guests, Polixenes and Camillo, come to spy, in their disguise, on the doings of Florizel. It would be monstrous to suppose that she speaks in a country dialect: on the contrary she commands the most perfectly educated accent; and her tone is that of a well bred young highbrow from Girton or Vassar welcoming distinguished guests to a college garden-party.

Per.　　　　　　　Sir, welcome;
It is my father's will I should take on me
The hostess-ship o' the day. You're welcome, sir.
Give me those flowers there, Dorcas. Reverend sirs,
For you there's rosemary and rue; these keep
Seeming and savour all the winter long:
Grace and rememberance be to you both,
And welcome to our shearing!

Pol.　　　　　　　Shepherdess
(A fair one are you) well you fit our ages
With flowers of winter.

Per.　　　　　　　Sir, the year growing ancient,
Not yet on summer's death nor on the birth
Of trembling winter, the fairest flowers o' the season
Are our carnations and streak'd gillivors,
Which some call nature's bastards: of that kind
Our rustic garden's barren; and I care not
To get slips of them.

Pol.　　　　　　　Wherefore, gentle maiden,
Do you neglect them?

Per.　　　　　　　For I have heard it said
There is an art which in their piedness shares
With great creating nature.

And Perdita's last remarks lead to quite a scholastic speech by Polixenes on the relation of nature and art. We have reached something as outrageous in its way as Spenser's Shepherd of the Ocean driving the seals to pasture. Perdita's breeding has, quite rightly, not worried readers, even modern ones. These have inherited enough of old traditions to take it for granted that in a romantic play, especially if it is written in verse, a born princess may behave as such even if in the actuality of her circumstances princely behaviour was out of the question. Thus the wild improbability has not even had to be pardoned, for it has escaped notice.

What conclusion then can we draw from Shakespeare's use of the Pastoral? Certainly not that he used exceptionally realistic methods for it. On the contrary he pursued his old habit of combining the plausible and the outrageous. He was extremely successful in using the characteristic Elizabethan method: a method which largely accounts for the glorious life and variety of the best literature of the Elizabethan age.

I have spoken of reality and fantasy in Elizabethan literature. But I do not wish to suggest that these two constitute the only Elizabethan paradox. And I will end by pointing to the largest of all: the belief in all the details and complications of life as lived on earth and yet the sense of their triviality in the setting of eternity. Raleigh, after enlarging on the joys of heaven which will make any earthly joys negligible, adds that this does not mean that honour and riches are to be despised or that the various hierarchies in mankind and in nature can be neglected. And when Shakespeare revived the old commonplace that all the world was a stage he enriched its meaning. In a way that stage was the Globe Theatre with its intense passionate happenings and with its great range of characters represented. But Shakespeare was aware of another dramatic picture: that of man, set in the theatre of nature in all its glory and multiplicity, acting out his part beneath the eye of heaven. Given a bitter turn, this second picture is presented by Coriolanus when he yields to his mother's plea to spare Rome:

> O mother, mother,
> What have you done? Behold, the heavens do ope,
> The gods look down and this unnatural scene
> They laugh at.

And it is as a part of this dramatic picture that we must consider Prospero's enumeration of

> The cloud-capped towers, the gorgeous palaces,
> The solemn temples, the great globe itself,

which shall dissolve and leave not a wrack behind. Only by recognising the double theatrical picture, the theatrical picture of man's varied activity and that picture as set in eternity, can we grasp the full scope of Shakespeare's conceptions of man acting out his destiny.

The Literary Kinds and Milton

I N spite of the good work done by Austin Warren, Kenneth
Burke, and Northrop Frye either in discussing or in de-
fining the literary kinds, I conjecture that interest in them
has never recovered from the efforts of Croce to show that in
any serious sense they are superfluous. Croce had no objection to using the traditional terms loosely as a vague signpost,
as long as it were understood that, scientifically, the only
valid unit was the individual work of art. With some people
Croce's view prevailed; but, even when it did not, it had the
effect of turning men's minds from the whole subject. Of
course people went on referring to literary kinds and forms,
and this they could not do without various tacit implications.
For instance, it was tacitly agreed that though a sonnet
should be judged ultimately for its value as an independent
piece of literature it was likely to have closer kinship with
other compositions in its own special metrical form than for
instance with a piece of prose fiction. And people would not
have continued naming the different literary kinds and forms
in speech and writing, as they have done, unless they had
thought it worth while doing so. But they have been care-
less of any principles governing the kinds or forms they refer
to; they have labelled certain literary phenomena sonnets
or pastorals or novels as if the reasons for such labels were
similar.

A moment's thought shows that these reasons have little
in common. Sonnets owe their first differentiation to metre,
pastorals to subject and characters, while novels are so
heterogeneous that no simple differentiation is possible. To
think of these as parallel literary kinds can only breed
confusion.

Let me suggest divisions within the general area of kinds
and forms truer to the facts than the common loose use of
which I have just complained.

First, there is the category of metre; and this is a safe

category. The sonnet, rondeau, ballade, limerick, etc., can be fairly closely defined; less closely, but not without all sense, the ode. And you are free to maintain that a rigid metrical form has some sway over the kind of sentiment it embodies. Thus Rossetti began a sonnet with the line, "A sonnet is a moment's monument."

Second, there is the category of nominal subject-matter. You can thus define a heroic poem as a composition in verse dealing with high action, pastoral as a composition about the doings and words of shepherds. Or, in the Middle Ages, you could define tragedy as a human action in which there was a change from good to ill estate. Here again we are safe enough; but at the cost of achieving little, for the range of essential character within the kinds as thus conceived is so vast as to rob the titles of any significance. Whatever the virtue of Statius's *Thebais* it has no affinity with that of Homer's *Iliad*, and to call them both epics in this sense of nominal heroic subject-matter gets you just nowhere.

Then there are the vague labels, admittedly vastly inclusive and useful enough in their unpretentious way: drama, verse narrative, prose fiction.

But you can think of the literary kinds in two much more important ways. You can think of certain areas of literature empirically as centres of convention, where tradition and the rules of the game matter very much indeed. We are here in the realm of chance and of history, of what actually did happen and not of what ought to happen. Examples are the Renaissance pastoral and in recent years detective fiction. These centres of convention are very important and they vary from age to age; though apart from the example cited they have ceased today to exist in any large way. But of their former power there is no doubt; and when I come to Milton I shall maintain that for him the literary forms were above all centres of convention.

Finally, I come to the only conception of the literary kinds that is likely to have an appeal today, namely the psychological one: that there are recurrent motions of the human mind and that literary kinds, in any profound sense, consist of the embodiments of these motions. Such a conception usually conflicts with other conceptions I have mentioned. Thus while under the second category you can put the unit of comedy in terms of a stage play that is more cheerful than sad and has a happy ending, you can also violate this description by saying that comedy deals whether dramatically or not with the eternal human theme of man's relation to society and his need to come to terms with it. Typical themes of comedy are that normal young men who forswear female society act foolishly and are not likely to keep their vows, that shrews ought to be disciplined, that swindlers or egoists cannot go on sucking the blood of society for ever, that even a most superior man risks becoming an outcast if he is too proud to recognise the standards of the ordinary middling person. And if these themes have been presented in successful plays, they could also be presented in narrative; and successful presentation in narrative would have the same right to fulfil the requirements of the comic as the successful presentation in drama. Comedy then has to do with a way of feeling and thinking.

To define the literary kinds thus psychologically is to incur all sorts of risks, is to leave restricted safety for a realm where conjecture has every chance of flourishing; and yet I hold that these risks must be run. If the literary kinds are to enjoy any vogue today, if they are to be living critical terms, they *must* be grounded on the facts of the human mind. I believe myself that this search for psychological grounds is stimulating, that it profits us to ask of the different literary labels whether they correspond to any facts of the human mind. The result must sometimes be that they will be found to correspond to more than one fact; that for instance it is useless to reduce the kind of tragedy to any one grand habit or posture of the mind. But I do not wish to embark on the topic of tragedy and instead I will point to two literary kinds; one so multifarious as to be almost meaningless, the other well rooted in essential human nature.

In its first efflorescence in Greece the pastoral may have corresponded to a genuine and recognisable human nostalgia; but later it became a mongrel. As a convention it was of great importance, but within the convention all sorts of psychological states could be subsumed. It could range from amorous triviality in a song to the high political earnestness of Sidney's *Arcadia* and the essentially tragic feeling of *Lycidas*. On the other hand the Dirge is a genuine, if simple, literary kind. There is a tacit human agreement that, at the moment of death and a little after, some sort of lamentation or regret is decent: more decent than frankness if death is welcome, or than silence if it is genuinely regretted. The Dirge is founded on these simple psychological facts.

I have indicated what seems to me the only way of looking at the literary kinds likely to be valid today largely to make really striking the totally different state of affairs prevailing in the age of Milton. The notion that the literary kinds can live only if they are found to correspond to some great recurrent motion of the human mind is simple in itself and must have been within the comprehension of an educated man of Milton's day if he could really heed it. But I do not believe he could have heeded it because it ignores what for him was the very life of the kinds, the very things that made them an attraction and an inspiration. For Milton the kinds were a set of conventions hallowed by tradition and ancient practice and the indispensable means of access to literary success; and as such they had so transcendent an importance that modern psychological theories of the kinds would have appeared superfluous or indeed blasphemous. Today, on the other hand, the dignity that hung over the abstract notions of epic, ode, or pastoral is dead. A writer may apply himself to the task of writing as well as possible with great seriousness, but that seriousness will be in no degree increased by the thought that he is working in one of the great traditional modes.

Not that the psychological way of regarding the literary kinds was unknown in Milton's day. It goes back to Aristotle; to his reasons why man is imitative and to his definition of tragedy in the *Poetics* and to the fundamental assumption in the *Rhetoric* that certain types of plea have their necessary response in the human mind. And Milton was well acquainted with Aristotle. But far more powerful was the almost mystical, Platonic way of regarding the kinds: of regarding them as essences laid up in some heavenly store and there awaiting the advent of some great writer to give them fit earthly embodiment. Further, some of the kinds *had* received fit embodiment and could serve both as models and as incentives to further endeavour. Once such embodiment had taken place, conventions about how thus to embody them were worked out and fixed and these were hallowed by tradition. Milton shows allegiance both to the Platonic notion of the kinds and to the notion of them as hallowed conventions, when in a famous passage in *Reason of Church Government* he lists the different kinds that might offer the right scope to his ambitions. These, he says, are "of highest hope and hardest attempting." The options are "that epic form whereof the two poems of Homer, and those other two of Virgil and Tasso, are a diffuse, and the Book of Job a brief model," next "those dramatic constitutions wherein Sophocles and Euripides reign," and he wonders whether or not these would be "found more doctrinal and exemplary to a nation" than epic. Then there is Scripture with its models of the Song of Solomon, "a divine pastoral drama", and the Apocalypse, "the majestic image of a high and stately tragedy." Last, there are "those magnific odes and hymns, wherein Pindarus and Callimachus are in most things worthy." Throughout the whole of the passage Milton is entirely possessed by the thought that the way to success lies through the willing and eager acceptance of the conventions that now governed the different literary kinds.

Consider for a moment the most famous of all the conventions governing a literary kind: the Three Dramatic Unities. Think first of the utter irrelevance of these to the modern notion that the kind of tragedy is based on one or more ever recurrent motions of the human mind. And then think of how they presented themselves to Milton: namely as a convention derived from antiquity and hallowed by the best precedent, the keeping of which was part of the surest way to the highest success; that is success before a superior international audience, with a view to glorifying your country in the eyes of the civilised world.

Let me try to bring out this utter change of conditions from Milton's to our own time by considering what Milton made of two traditional literary kinds, the pastoral and the epic.

Milton wrote four pastoral poems: *Arcades*, *Comus*, *Lycidas*, and *Epitaphium Damonis*. *Arcades* is an aristocratic entertainment, gay but with undertones of seriousness, nicely calculated to grace an evening's relaxation. Messrs Brooks and Hardy would persuade us that the migration of the Arcadian shepherds to a new home in England, which is the slender plot of the masque, signifies Milton's claim that the pastoral can flourish better in England than in its Mediterranean birth-place. There is nothing improbable in the actual claim—later, in his poem to Manso, Milton was to defend the poetical eminence of his country, *Nos etiam colimus Phoebum*—but I do not myself find it arising naturally from the context. But even if the claim is there it does not make *Arcades* anything other than what I have called it, an aristocratic entertainment. *Comus*, on the other hand, though nominally of the same kind as *Arcades*, is less an entertainment than a grave moral allegory, founded on the traditional allegorical significance implicit in the legend of Circe and the transformation of the companions of Odysseus into beasts. The ground meaning of *Lycidas*, in spite of its scrupulous following of the details of the classical pastoral dirge, is purely tragic; it renders the predicament of the individual in the universe. Lastly *Epitaphium Damonis* is the effusion of a sincere personal grief. It is far the most intimate personal poem Milton wrote; and we may guess that he would have hesitated to write or rather publish it had he not mitigated the personal tone by writing in an alien language.

Whether or not I have described the four poems aright, at least I must have made it clear that though nominally united by their pastoral guise they correspond each to a different place in the human mind. By a modern criterion the word *pastoral* as applied to them is very nearly nonsense. On the other hand, to Milton it meant a very great deal. It meant first that by writing these early poems in a pastoral guise he was following the lead of the poets he most admired and whom he most wished to emulate: Virgil, Tasso, Spenser. Indeed, the right routine for the poet who aspired to the highest reaches of poetry was to begin with the pastoral or some minor form of didactic verse. The use of the pastoral for Milton meant the happy conviction that whether or not he was destined to arrive he was on the right path for his journey. And quite apart from the future there is the effect of such assurance on the actual poems, and that effect was beneficial. When in *Lycidas* Milton makes the different characters come to join the lamentation he is utterly assured that he is doing the right thing; there is not the least sense of his forcing it, of his being self-consciously correct: on the contrary, reposing in the convention he feels himself to be doing the most natural thing in the world. And last, through following the pastoral convention, Milton found himself in the area of competition: he saw himself striving in friendly and fruitful rivalry with the greatest. The very convention constituted a challenge.

Before going on to the epic form I would note that it is to these conventions of which I am speaking that Brunetière's theory of the *évolution des genres* best applies. For instance the conventional status of the verse epic, tinged with Platonic mysticism, and exalted through its exploitation by the two poets then considered the greatest of all and through the added idea that by its means you could on the literary side best serve your country, could not remain unchanged. It had reached such a pitch through a gradual evolution; it could not but suffer a decline. It is also worth noting that Brunetière's book on the kinds also contains the germ of the psychological way of considering them. For instance, he advances the notion of transformation, seeing in the lyric poetry of Lamartine, Hugo, Vigny, and Musset the transformation of the pulpit eloquence of the seventeenth century in France. Surely this implies that the eloquence corresponded to something in the human mind and that this thing found a transformed expression in the lyric. But Brunetière unfortunately does not explain.

Even more than the pastoral the epic kind provided Milton with a challenge, and a tremendous challenge perfectly suited to get the best out of his ardent and persevering nature. Its effect was wholly for the good. And yet the epic convention left him a freedom comparable with the freedom he enjoyed within the pastoral. Since Milton wrote but two epics, we have not the same means of judging as with his pastorals. But *Paradise Regained* differs markedly in temper from *Paradise Lost*; and we can conjecture with some probability about what he would have made of his epic on Arthur, had conditions permitted his writing it. It would have been bellicose and would have followed the precedents mentioned in *Reason of Church Government*, Homer Virgil Tasso, pretty closely. It would have been patriotic and as Protestant as Tasso's *Jerusalem* was Catholic. That Milton, when at last he composed his epics, could abandon these characteristics shows the wide freedom the epic kind allowed him. In its main lines *Paradise Lost* forsook the precedent of the bellicose epic. It is closer in structure to the least bellicose of the great epics, the *Odyssey*, and for its protagonists it forsook the classical heroes for the medieval Everyman. Its crowning boldness was to make Adam and Eve homely as well as stately and typical of Man and Woman. In fact, Milton effected within one of the most pompous and apparently strict literary conventions a change not unlike that effected on art by the French Impressionists: the change from a public, official art to the unofficial subtleties of a new kind of landscape.

Thus Milton did enjoy freedom of a sort; but how different a sort from that current today! The difference is as great as that between Milton's conception and the modern psychological conception of the literary kinds. But it was the sort of freedom he believed in: the willing or enthusiastic acquiescence in a set of conventions ratified by reason and hallowed by the experience of ages.

Finally, Milton's conception of the kinds was valuable because it worked. Vulnerable on the critical side, it furthered the creation of literature. The psychological conception of the kinds is critically far sounder, but hitherto it has had not the least influence on creation. But it is new, and may be at some future date writers will find it helps them to see clearly what particular part of the mind they want predominantly to colour and characterise the work they propose to undertake.

A Note on Dryden's Criticism[1]

LITERARY criticism, when it rises to excellence, is usually scrappy or elusive. The scrappy kind consists of aphorisms or of brilliant brief perceptions of great literature; and Longinus and Coleridge are two of its practitioners. The elusive kind owes its greatness less to the separate perceptions than to a spirit or disposition that arises from the sum of the parts. And that spirit is apt to elude definition. Horace and Boileau, so little interesting from their separate perceptions, are great in this way. And of course one kind does not exclude the other.

It is generally agreed that Dryden is among the greatest literary critics. But when we ask in what his greatness consists, the answer is not easy. And the reason is not so much that we lack the materials for an answer as that we cannot easily see the shape of them; the very abundance of excellence embarrasses. Of course, if we confined Dryden's critical greatness to the first of the two kinds I have mentioned, to his power of throwing out, amidst much that is conventional, an abundance of fine critical perceptions, we should not find him hard to place. But his greatness is so much more than that, for it is of that second kind also; a scent, as it were, pervading and distinguishing nearly all his work. It is indeed right to seek to enumerate his critical perceptions; and doubtless some general truths would emerge from such an enumeration. But, unlike some critics, he does not really thrive by anthologising; and nothing but the whole does justice to his inmost critical disposition.

Attempts to define that disposition are not lacking. Saintsbury[2] ranges Dryden's critical excellence under three headings: in the last analysis Dryden, unshackled by the rules, judged literature as he found it; next he took technical

[1] Copyright 1951 by the Board of Trustees of the Leland Stanford Junior University.

[2] *A History of Criticism* (3rd ed., Edinburgh, 1914), ii, 373-4.

questions seriously; and last he believed that poetry *must* delight. Now Saintsbury may be correct in all these contentions; but they apply to Edith Sitwell, for instance, equally with Dryden. And though Edith Sitwell is a good critic in her very individual way, she is not at all like Dryden. So Saintsbury has not characterised Dryden very sharply. W. P. Ker wrote more precisely:

> Dryden's power as a writer of criticism does not depend upon his definite judgements. . . . His virtue is that in a time when literature was pestered and cramped with formulas he found it impossible to write otherwise than freely. He is sceptical, tentative, disengaged, where most of his contemporaries, and most of his successors for a hundred years, are pledged to certain dogmas and principles.[1]

Ker's words about Dryden's scepticism and freedom are excellent as far as they go. But they are on the negative side; and surely his first sentence is mistaken, unless by "definite judgements" he means no more than Dryden's fairly frequent iteration of certain commonplaces of critical theory generally accepted in his day. Anyhow, the attempt to carry an assessment of Dryden's general critical powers beyond Ker is worth making.

First let me correct Ker's first sentence by saying that Dryden made definite judgements on certain authors and that some of those judgements are admirable, exhibiting considerable "power" in Dryden "as a writer of criticism." As it is fairly long, one instance will suffice. It is his judgement on Lucretius from the preface to *Sylvae*:

> The distinguishing character of Lucretius (I mean of his soul and genius) is a certain kind of noble pride and positive assertion of his opinions. He is everywhere confident of his own reason and assuming an absolute command, not only over his vulgar reader, but even his patron Memmius. For he is always bidding him attend, as if he had the rod over him; and using a magisterial authority, while he instructs him . . . Lucretius . . . seems to disdain all manner of replies and is so confident of his cause, that

[1] *Essays of John Dryden* (Oxford, 1900), i, xv.

he is beforehand with his antagonists; urging for them whatever he imagined they could say, and leaving them, as he supposes, without an objection for the future. All this too with so much scorn and indignation, as if he were assured of the triumph, before he entered into the lists. From this sublime and daring genius of his, it must of necessity come to pass that his thoughts must be masculine, full of argumentation, and that sufficiently warm. From the same fiery temper proceeds the loftiness of his expressions and the perpetual torrent of his verse, where the barrenness of his subject does not too much constrain the quickness of his fancy. For there is no doubt to be made but that he could have been everywhere as poetical as he is in his descriptions and in the moral part of his philosophy, if he had not aimed more to instruct, in his system of Nature, than to delight. But he was bent upon making Memmius a materialist and teaching him to defy an invisible power: in short, he was so much an atheist, that he forgot sometimes to be a poet.[1]

Casting my mind back on a now distant classical education and trying to recollect the kind of thing that was said about Lucretius, I register the faint impression of an old-fashioned poet superb (and better than Virgil) in some purple patches, but to be read in between those patches not because you would want to read him but because, as a classic, you must read him. No one ever told me that Dryden had written of Lucretius, but what an inspiration that writing would have been and what a contrast Dryden's majestic seizing of the vital generalities would have made to the feeble picking on the surface I have described! Dryden goes straight to the animating principles; he sees that the plastic stress of Lucretius's passionate imagination tortured some but not all of the dross in his system of nature into the form he desired, but he sees that Lucretius leaves the intractable part interesting, that it is no mere series of dreary flats in between the exciting elevations and that it is livingly if imperfectly related to the centre of his genius. Now such success in grasping the general properties of a work of art and expressing them clearly and emphatically argues the highest

1 Ker, *op. cit.*, i, 259-60.

critical power. And the passages where Dryden thus succeeds could be multiplied. He qualifies for critical greatness as being a writer from whose works could be compiled a critical scrap-book of the highest distinction.

Omitting other grounds for his critical excellence I revert to the question whether out of Dryden's critical writing there emerges any one positive principle that projects above any other emergent principles and constitutes his proper critical genius. I believe there is and I will try to describe it.

Brunetière considered that Boileau was a great critic because he substituted Reason for the Ancients as the authority for literary judgements. In other words Boileau did for literature what Descartes did for philosophy: he grounded his belief not on ancient received opinion but on the dictates of the human mind. And just as Descartes reached the same conclusion on the existence of God that authority had demanded, so Boileau accepted, by however different a route, the main tenets of neo-classicism. The point, however, is that Boileau had achieved a new freedom, for, if he had found Reason and the Ancients at odds, he could have rejected the Ancients. Dryden, highly sensitive to the happenings of his age, was open to this new Cartesian freedom. He probably derived most of his knowledge of Descartes from talk with his learned acquaintance, in the manner described so masterly by Johnson in his *Life of Dryden*. That he knew the most famous detail of Cartesianism and that he knew his audience to be familiar with it appears from the way he adapted an episode in *Paradise Lost* to his own uses in the *State of Innocence*. In *Paradise Lost* Adam's first conscious act after creation was to "turn his wondering eyes toward heaven." He then scanned the landscape, found he could name the things he saw, asked the natural objects around him if they could tell "how came I thus, how here," and, answering his own question, concluded:

> Not of my self; by some great Maker then,
> In goodness and in power prae-eminent.

At the beginning of the second act of the *State of Innocence*

Adam is discovered "as newly created, laid on a bed of moss and flowers, by a rock." His first words are:

> What am I? or from whence? for that I am
> I know, because I think,

after which he concludes that there is a divine power, from which he comes. Unlike Milton's, Dryden's Adam begins from within himself, from the doctrine that thought proves existence, according to the then novel philosophy of Descartes.

Dryden then knew Descartes and was free to profit by Descartes' initial scepticism.[1] And profit he did in a way very different from Boileau. While Boileau was mainly concerned with rebuilding the old principles on new and better foundations, Dryden used his new option to turn a highly inquisitive and absorbed, but perfectly impartial, eye on all the literature (and it was extensive) that interested him. Freed from a superstitious regard for the Ancients, he used his skill to look at them quite coolly and with no more initial respect than he accorded to the writers of his own day. The result is a perfection of *tone* in matters of comparative literature that has not been equalled before or since. And this is his paramount critical achievement.

Dryden did not reach perfection of tone at once. There is something rather set and formal about the way he treats Ancients, French, and English in the *Essay of Dramatic Poesy*, as if he were arguing for freedom and impartiality, not taking them serenely for granted. But from the *Author's Apology for Heroic Poetry* (1677) onwards the tone is perfect. Take this from the preface to *Troilus and Cressida* on the different dramatists' skill in giving a king his true character:

> Sophocles gives to Oepidus the true qualities of a king, in both those plays which bear his name; but in the latter, which is the Oepidus Colonaeus, he lets fall on purpose his tragic style; his hero speaks not in the arbitrary tone; but remembers in the soft-

[1] Dryden knew his own freedom. See his *Defence of the Epilogue* (Ker, *op. cit.*, i, 163): "For we live in an age so sceptical, that as it determines little, so it takes nothing from antiquity on trust."

ness of his complaints, that he is an unfortunate blind old man; that he is banished from his country, and persecuted by his next relations. The present French poets are generally accused, that wheresoever they lay the scene, or in whatsoever age, the manners of their heroes are wholly French. Racine's Bajazet is bred at Constantinople; but his civilities are conveyed to him, by some secret passage, from Versailles into the Seraglio. But our Shakespeare, having ascribed to Henry the Fourth the character of a king and of a father, gives him the perfect manners of each relation, when either he transacts with his son or with his subjects.[1]

Dryden may be unfair here to Racine, but, if so, it is not the critical tone that is wrong but the criticism itself.

There was another reason than Descartes why Dryden should have been able to speak in one and the same tone of Sophocles and Shakespeare, of Virgil and Milton. By living when he did he escaped the idolatry with which the Classics were invested both before and after his age. At its outset the Renaissance enthusiasm for the Classics was too lively and noble to be called idolatry, but it could easily degenerate into a dead and uncritical acceptance. Against such an acceptance Dryden did not need to fight; its day was over. Nor had there yet arisen the much more selective and pedantic idolatry that reached its climax in the Public Schools and ancient Universities of nineteenth century England and Ireland. To speak more specifically, scholars and teachers had not then agreed to call a selection of Greek and Latin authors correct, on account of the supposed purity of the language they used, and to make the writing of *pastiche* of these authors one of the absolute values of life. Dryden could think of Statius as just Statius and not as a Silver Latin, and hence rather suspect, poet; while at Westminster School and at Cambridge he wrote original, if not correctly Augustan, Latin, and did not have to translate small passages of English prose laboriously into the closest possible imitation of one of the authorised classical prosaists. This later idolatry may have served an educational purpose, but it did not

[1]Ker, *op. cit.*, i, 217-18.

promote a true critical tone. Nineteenth century criticism of the Classics cannot touch the quality of Dryden's.

Lastly, Dryden not only achieved a perfect critical tone, he made a full use of the freedom on which that tone was based. He did in fact criticise authors in a number of different ways, as the spirit moved him. I shall not attempt to enumerate those ways, but shall confine myself to citing one which was very original in his day and to which I have not come across any tribute. It is the longish passage in the *Dedication of the Aeneis* where he explains on historical grounds why Virgil was justified in writing so political a poem as the *Aeneid*. In order to make quite clear how Virgil stood to Augustus, Dryden rapidly reviews the main political events in which Marius, Sulla, and the two Triumvirates were the actors. And this is the conclusion he reaches:

Virgil having maturely weighed the condition of the times in which he lived; that an entire liberty was not to be retrieved; that the present settlement had the prospect of a long continuance in the same family, or those adopted into it; that he held his paternal estate from the bounty of the conqueror, by whom he was likewise enriched, esteemed and cherished; that this conqueror, though of a bad kind, was the very best of it; that the arts of peace flourished under him; that all men might be happy if they would be quiet; that, now he was in possession of the whole, yet he shared a great part of his authority with the Senate; that he would be chosen into the ancient offices of the Commonwealth, and ruled by the power which he derived from them; and prorogued his government from time to time, still, as it were, threatening to dismiss himself from public cares, which he exercised more for the common good than for any delight he took in greatness; these things, I say, being considered by the poet, he concluded it to be the interest of his country to be so governed; to infuse an awful respect into the people towards such a prince; by that respect to confirm their obedience to him, and by that obedience to make them happy. This was the moral of his divine poem; honest in the poet; honourable to the Emperor, whom he derives from a divine extraction; and reflecting part of that honour on the Roman people, whom he derives also from the Trojans; and not only profitable, but necessary, to the present age, and likely to be such to their posterity.[1]

This is surely a most remarkable exercise of the historical imagination in the interest of critical truth and quite surprising in the age where it occurs: the fruit at once of the freedom Dryden enjoyed and of his own incomparably fresh and inquiring critical spirit.

But, the reader may ask, was Dryden being original? Have not Saintsbury and Ker told us that Dryden's three long essays, on satire, on painting and poetry, and on the *Aeneid* are inferior works, rather laboured and clogged with borrowed learning, though enlivened by many original touches of detail? In particular, the *Dedication of the Aeneis* is said to derive largely from Segrais. Now, it is perilous to assert that any passage in seventeenth-century criticism is not stolen from another. But at least I can assert that the passage under discussion reads uncommonly fresh, as if it issued straight from the deep knowledge Dryden had acquired of the *Aeneid* in translating it and the passionate interest that knowledge bred. And as for Segrais, Dryden mostly acknowledges his debts (modest enough) as they occur, and for a source of Dryden's long discourse on history the following is the only possible passage that could come into question:

Virgile se trouva sujet d'Auguste, il vescut pendant la splendeur de l'Empire Romain dans le siecle le plus poly, le plus delicat, et le plus juste qui ait jamais esté dans toute la durée de la langue Latine: Il passa sa vie sous le regne d'un Prince qui le combla de richesses, et qui a esté l'un des plus grands hommes qu'on puisse proposer aux autres pour example. . . . Aprés avoir achevé ses Eglogues et son Poëme de la vie rustique . . . il crût que pour monter à la plus haute reputation ou puisse aspirer un Poëte, il fallait exceller dans le genre sublime, comme il avoit fait dans les deux autres; et concevoir en mesme temps un ouvrage qui fust honorable à son Auteur et à sa Patrie; et qui témoignast sa reconnaissance envers son Prince.[2]

[1] Ker, *op. cit.*, ii, 171-2.
[2] *Traduction de L'Eneide de Virgile par Mr de Segrais* (Paris, 1668), i, 7-8.

And Segrais goes on to say that the reader must put himself into the changed position of the age in which a poet writes. And even if this was the hint Dryden took up in writing of the historical background of the *Aeneid*, his treatment is so ample and so far transcends anything in Segrais that it is virtually original.

It would be possible greatly to enlarge on the theme of Dryden's positive achievements in criticism, but I hope I have said enough to show that not only was Dryden "sceptical, tentative, disengaged" but that out of this scepticism and disengaged, experimental criticism there emerged a free critical disposition which was both admirable in itself and which achieved positive results of a very high quality.

William Collins's "Ode on the Death of Thomson"

1. In yonder grave a Druid lies,
    Where slowly winds the stealing wave!
  The year's best sweets shall duteous rise
    To deck its poet's sylvan grave!

2. In yon deep bed of whisp'ring reeds
    His airy harp shall now be laid,
  That he, whose heart in sorrow bleeds,
    May love through life the soothing shade.

3. Then maids and youths shall linger here,
    And while its sounds at distance swell,
  Shall sadly seem in Pity's ear
    To hear the woodland pilgrim's knell.

4. Remembrance oft shall haunt the shore
    When Thames in summer weeds is drest,
  And oft suspend the dashing oar
    To bid his gentle spirit rest.

5. And oft as Ease and Health retire
    To breezy lawn or forest deep,
  The friend shall view yon whitening spire,
    And 'mid the varied landscape weep.

6. But thou, that own'st that earthy bed,
    Ah! what will every dirge avail?
  Or tears, which Love and Pity shed,
    That mourn beneath the gliding sail?

7. Yet lives there one, whose heedless eye
    Whall scorn thy pale shrine glimm'ring near?
  With him, sweet bard, may fancy die,
    And joy desert the blooming year.

8. But thou, lorn stream, whose sullen tide
   No sedge-crown'd sisters now attend,
   Now waft me from the green hill's side,
   Whose cold turf hides the buried friend!

9. And see, the fairy valleys fade,
   Dun Night has veil'd the solemn view.
   Yet once again, dear parted shade,
   Meek Nature's child, again adieu!

10. The genial meads assign'd to bless
    Thy life, shall mourn thy early doom;
    Their hinds and shepherd-girls shall dress
    With simple hands thy rural tomb.

11. Long, long, thy stone and pointed clay
    Shall melt the musing Briton's eyes;
    O vales and wild woods, shall he say,
    In yonder grave your Druid lies!

THE explicators have largely spared the poetry of the eighteenth century; and the reason is not far to seek. The poetry they favour is either difficult to construe or rich in multiple meanings. Some of Donne's *Songs and Sonnets* have exactly the right, the most attractive, amount of difficulty; some of Hopkins's lyrics (to judge by a recent correspondence in the *Times Literary Supplement* on the word *buckle* in the *Windhover*) yield the most abundant semantic ramifications. The poetry of the eighteenth century is different; its superficial sense hits us at once; and it aims at clarity, not suggestiveness. It thus eludes the concern dearest to the hearts of the explicators. All the same, we today cannot easily perceive and enjoy that clarity which was its first aim.

One reason is that we hold different opinions about the general and the particular in poetry. Blake said that to generalise was the sign of an idiot; and his doctrine prevailed with the Romantics, even surviving the reaction against Romanticism in recent years. Johnson, we still hold, was wrong when he advanced the doctrine of the general, of not numbering the streaks of the tulip; and Shakespeare was right in conveying the atmospheric stillness at the opening of *Hamlet* by the detail "Not a mouse stirring." Further, we hold, the eighteenth century went astray because of its belief in decorum. For instance it ruled that you must not use the technical terms of any craft in polite writing because you thereby consorted with a base section of society and puzzled the mass of educated readers who, quite rightly, were not acquainted with the special craft.

Later ages may have done well to follow Blake; but in doing so they oversimplified the issue, ignoring what the current generalities meant to the eighteenth-century reader. To him these were not *merely* decorous or politely remote from real things; they were natural and they were alive. And a prime task of anyone who seeks to explicate eighteenth-century poetry is to restore to the general statements, the polite epithets, and the personifications the life which in the best literature they once possessed. It is a task as irrelevant to Donne or Hopkins as it is relevant to this poem of Collins. In discussing it I shall have first to show how much detail he conceals in his general elegiac statements and how forceful some of it is.

Collins wrote for educated readers, and he assumed that they had read Thomson's best poems, the *Seasons* and the *Castle of Indolence*. He also tells us in a footnote that the "whit'ning spire" is that of Richmond church, which borders on the Thames. And we too should know so much before entering the poem. Not that this knowledge prevents queer things happening the moment we do enter it.

The modern reader is not averse to the first stanza's dramatic pointing to the newly dug grave; but the use of the word *Druid* for *poet* does not help him to create a dramatic picture. On the contrary the word looks like a piece of chill pseudo-politeness, an unfortunate attempt to exalt the subject of the elegy by a dragged-in piece of antiquarianism. But this appearance is deceptive. The eighteenth-century reader *expected* politeness, not to say pomp, while the word *Druid* had certain associations for him. The Druid was essentially a bard: Milton in *Lycidas* had written of "the steep, Where your old *Bards*, the famous *Druids*, lie," and, six years after Collins's ode, Gray had begun the *Bard*, founded on the legend that Edward I had put the bards or Druids of Wales to death. By calling Thomson a Druid Collins placed him among the classic poets of the land and hinted, through the traditional connection of the Druids with the oak-tree, at Thomson's eminence as the poet of nature; a hint taken up in the second half of the verse where "the year's best sweets," that is the loveliest flowers or foliage of the four seasons, are pictured as offering themselves to adorn his grave. Again, to a modern reader "the year's best sweets" is at first reading as chilly as the Druid; but Collins meant it to be a signal for the imagination to go further and to picture the various seasonal offerings. The first verse is neither tame nor conventional. On the contrary it is violent in the way it aggregates the flowers and proclaims their spontaneous self-sacrifice to the man who celebrated them so well in his poem called the *Seasons*.

From the *Seasons* Collins goes on in the next verse to the *Castle of Indolence*, brought in through his allusion to the Aeolian harp, the subject of one of that poem's most famous stanzas. In the fabled Castle of Indolence the characteristic music was passive, that of the Aeolian harp, which, sounding when blown on, gave out different music according to the volume and quality of the wind.

> A certain music, never known before,
> Here lulled the pensive, melancholy mind;
> Full easily obtain'd. Behoves no more,
> But sidelong, to the gently-waving wind,
> To lay the well-tuned instrument reclined;
> From which, with airy flying fingers light,
> Beyond each mortal touch the most refined,
> The God of Winds drew sounds of deep delight:
> Whence, with just cause, the Harp of Aeolus it hight.

It is to this stanza that Collins refers in his second verse where the even lapse of the words tempts us again to slur over the concreteness of the setting and the precision of thought. We should picture the actual reeds bordering the tomb and the river and deduce the plain meaning that the lovely music of the *Castle of Indolence* will be the perpetual delight of sensitive people.

The third verse turns from specific literary reference to more general sorrow. The harp, sounding with the wind from the reeds, will awaken in the tender hearts of the young a feeling of sorrow for Thomson's death.

The next two verses are still more particularised, but in the true eighteenth-century way of polite personification. They mean that in summer time many people who like to remember Thomson will pass the place by river and cause the rowers to row slowly or "easy," in reverence of his gentle ghost; other admirers, who prefer a land excursion for health and relaxation, will see the spire of Richmond church and lament him. He will, in fact, be a kind of classical hero, attracting votaries to his tomb. When Collins said "Remembrance oft shall haunt the shore," he was using a polite personification, but he was also being definite, meaning by *Remembrance* "reminiscent people," just as Goldsmith in the line "For talking Age and whispering lovers made," meant by *talking Age* "garrulous old folk." Similarly by "Ease and Health" Collins means healthy people taking a holiday. If we fail to translate these personified qualities into imagined men and women and to fuse them in the picture we also fail in the sympathy necessary for understanding the poem.

The remaining verses are less formal. Collins, growing more impassioned in the sixth and seventh verses, laments that the tears of his admirers do the dead poet no good and curses any wretch who slights him. There follow two verses describing the river, now deserted as night falls. Nature asserts itself in fact; and the "hinds and shepherd-girls" who in the next stanza "dress" Thomson's "rural tomb" are true country-folk and not sophisticated visitors from neighbouring London. Those who live nearest to nature are the fittest to commemorate nature's poet. Yet Thomson was a national figure, and in the last verse it is the "musing Briton," the educated inhabitants of the British Isles, who corporately should honour him; and in the last line Collins calls him a "Druid" once more. (What, incidentally, does "pointed clay" mean in the first line of the last stanza, "Long, long, thy stone, and pointed clay"? I think it is a latinism and means the indication of the body's resting-place, *point* being sometimes used in Collins's day for *point out* or *indicate*.)

So far, discussed in this way, the poem does not amount to more than a conventional elegy composed of inherited elements: praise of the dead poet's works, the visit of survivors to the tomb, lamentation for his death, and the hope of fame; all made agreeable by the liquid lapse of the verse. And yet I get the impression of there being more in the poem than this; and H. W. Garrod, Collins's sympathetic and understanding critic, confirmed it when he wrote, "I am left with a perplexed sense that this is a better poem than I seem to have allowed. . . . It is hard to define its obscure excellence." Such an impression applies to people as well as to poems. There is some hidden element in a person, which baffles you. Then perhaps you learn that he is an orphan, or an Irishman, or had a French mother, or was brought up in South America; and the extrinsic piece of information helps you to make a right beginning, and you have an unexpected entry into an interesting character. I welcome any extrinsic help in understanding poetry provided that in a final reading it escapes conscious notice. Now John Langhorne, a minor poet who edited Collins's verse in 1765, informs us that Collins's ode was "written in an excursion to Richmond by water." Given the hint we should perceive that we have to do with verses patterned on an actual river-excursion, that they compose a piece of water-music. The liquid lapse of the lines is that of the boat's glide through the water, and there is what can almost be called a plot in the way they hint at the boat's progress. One kind of progress has already been implied; that of gathering twilight. The tower of Richmond church is "whit'ning"; it catches the last rays of the sun; and later the "fairy valleys fade" and "Dim Night has veiled the solemn view." There is thus a double progression: that of nightfall and that of the boat on the river.

Let me now fill in the picture. The boat has an easy course, for it moves with the current, the stream in verse eight "wafting" the poet from "the green hill's side." And the motion is continuous; the crew does not land. The "plot" of the ode is that of the poet and his fellows in the boat sighting the grave in the evening light, being carried past it, and losing sight of it again as night falls. In the first line, "In yonder grave a Druid lies," *yonder* points forward. In the last line, "In yonder grave your Druid lies," *yonder* looks back. And there are hints throughout of the boat's distance from Thomson's grave. In verse three the harp's sound swells *at distance*. The next verse, which talks of "suspending the dashing oar," suggests that the boat is now nearer and goes slower to prolong the culminating moment. In the sixth verse the boat has arrived opposite the grave: in "that earthy bed" *that* has replaced the previous *yon's*, and the sentiment is, as explained, more passionate, concerned with the poet rather than with those who mourn him. In the seventh verse the tomb is "glimmering near." In the eighth the poet bids the stream carry the boat away from the tomb. But beyond these informative hints Collins re-creates with rare art the feelings one has in seeing an object grow near and then again grow distant. As one approaches, the interest thickens, one wishes to crowd in all possible items of sensation; as one looks back and sees the object dwindle, one despairs of such a thickening and relaxes in sympathy with the losing game. There are eleven verses in the poem. The first five concern the approaching boat and they are more crowded with information and with formality. (The first two verses incidentally are packed with sibilants and incurred thereby the censure of Lord Tennyson.) The middle verse is the culmination. The last five verses are more purely elegiac or descriptive, expressing a simpler sadness and a mood of relaxation. The ode's development thus agrees exquisitely with the experience of approaching and leaving an attractive object.

The last line of all, nearly repeating the first, is brilliant, packed with meaning after the fashion of only the greatest poetry. The first line of the poem, "In *yonder* grave a Druid lies," should be read with the stress on *yonder*, denoting expectancy. The last line, "In yonder *grave* your Druid lies," should be read with the stress on *grave*. The boat has passed; night has fallen; *yonder* is no longer emphatic; and the gathering dark has brought closer the thought of the grave. And through substituting *your Druid* for *a Druid* of line one (*your* referring to the vales and woods) Collins transfers Thomson from his own fostering care, shown earlier in the poem, to those natural things whose poet Thomson was and which belong to the earth in which he is buried. And to this transference the falling music of the last verse is perfectly appropriate.

My last observation is rasher and more conjectural. The richest lyrics usually reveal some contrast or paradox, doing justice to both constituent elements. In this ode of Collins there may be a contrast, larger than the context of the poem, between the human solicitude for Thomson and his memory, shown while the boat approaches, and the natural things, night and the earth, which are felt to envelop him while the boat recedes. It is the opposition between the human, the known, the particular and the natural, the unknown, the illimitable. In fact the poem may resolve itself into one of those large commonplaces that lie at the heart of most good poetry.

It was the habit, in the years when the Romantic poets were thought the norm of the centrally poetical, to talk of Gray and Collins as writers not belonging to that age, to picture them as eccentric individuals who did not fit in with its poetic conventions and its social exigencies. In fact, they were turned into precursors of the great flowering that was about to break forth. Of the two, Collins was the more eccentric and individual, though not necessarily the better poet. And of his poems the *Ode to Evening* was the remotest from the eighteenth century, supremely daring as an unrhymed lyric in the age of the couplet, and Wordsworthian in its steady contemplation of the natural scene:

> Or if chill blust'ring winds, or driving rain,
> Prevent my willing feet, be mine the hut,
> That from the mountain's side
> Views wilds and swelling floods,

And hamlets brown and dim-discover'd spires,
And hears their simple bell and ·marks o'er all
Thy dewy fingers draw
The gradual dusky veil.

It could only have been mistaken kindness that detached such lines from their age: the kindness of refusing to allow anything so sensitively pictorial to belong to an age of prose. And how mistaken! For the retired, the contemplative man, in this context the man who seeks his lonely hut, was part of the very mythology of the Augustan age, while the brown landscape is all of a piece with Thomson's *Seasons* and the nature painters in water-colours. The metre appeared alien to its age for a longer time: in fact till Garrod pointed out its unimpeachable decorum: unimpeachable because derived from Milton's translation of Horace's *Ode to Pyrrha*:

What slender youth bedew'd with liquid odours
Courts thee on roses in some pleasant cave,
Pyrrha, for whom bind'st thou
In wreaths thy golden hair?

Collins is indeed a man of his age; and not least in his relation to his audience. Johnson found "his appearance decent and manly; his knowledge considerable, his views extensive, his conversation elegant, and his disposition cheerful." And if later Collins was afflicted with a melancholy that for a time confined him to an asylum, Johnson never dreams of attributing the least particle of the cause to a feeling of hostility to his surroundings. Johnson says that he "employed his mind chiefly upon works of fiction and subjects of fancy, and, by indulging some peculiar habits of thought, was eminently delighted with those flights of imagination which pass the bounds of nature." But Johnson had no objection to some poetry behaving in this way, and he balances this description of Collins's mental proclivities by asserting that he "was a man of extensive literature and of vigorous faculties."

Collins, in fact, fully shares the obligation felt by his age

G

to consider the tastes and the requirements of the reading public.

Whatever the virtues, or the limitations, of Collins's *Ode Occasioned by the Death of Mr Thomson*, it is at ease with its audience, making its surprises or uniquenesses grow out of the poetical habits with which his equals were familiar, and well content to be read and enjoyed should its public consider it to be worth perusal and enjoyment.

Scott's Linguistic Vagaries

To set forth and account for Scott's varied use of language would need specialised erudition and the compass of a substantial book. I have neither the equipment nor the inclination to meet these two needs. All I seek to do is to note that the language of Scott's novels has been taken for granted with surprising coolness and to call attention to some of its strangeness. I shall illustrate mainly by the *Monastery*, linguistically far the strangest of the novels, and through such illustration I may comment incidentally on the progress or degeneration of Scott's fictional art.

The Waverley Novels succeeded so suddenly and overwhelmingly that they quickly became classics and models. Men took them as one of the great fictional norms and found them natural rather than strange. Natural they may have been compared with the run of Neo-Gothic fiction, but in some ways they are strange: strange in their play from the superficial to the profound, strange in the way their author caused them to yield to public opinion, strange in the disorder of their linguistic elements.

The linguistic pattern of Scott's first Scottish novels, that is of the series from *Waverley* to *A Legend of Montrose*, is indeed pretty clear. He used a contemporary English idiom, inherited from the eighteenth century, for description, narrative, and the speech of the more educated, and Lowland Scots for the speech of the humbler folk. In his English he uses an occasional "Ay" or "'Tis" if he wishes to stress an earlier date or feels melodramatically inclined, but he is always near his natural inheritance. Behind him we find Johnson, Horace Walpole (Gothic or ungothic), Hume, Mrs Radcliffe, and so on. Now he will remind us of Goldsmith's limpidity, now of Clara Reeve's sententiousness, but he does nothing to surprise us, except in the wonderful use to which he puts the different parts of his inheritance.

Scott's difficulties began with *Ivanhoe*, and he recognised them. Having exchanged Scotland for England and the post-Restoration period for the early Middle Ages, he could not continue as before. What emerges from the Dedicatory Epistle is first an uneasy feeling of conscience that he ought to archaise quite considerably and second the conviction that if he did as he ought he would be unreadable, like Chatterton. He defended an "unnatural" modernisation on the plea that elements common to medieval English and the English of his own day were far larger than was generally supposed: actually nine-tenths of the whole. But though he acted on this defence through much of *Ivanhoe*, his conscience insisted on a minimum of archaism; and to satisfy it he made his characters talk fitfully a language which has been described as "Wardour Street," "Tushery," or "Ye Olde." They are not consistent in its use, but they incline to affect it when they are being highminded or in a situation near the comic. And the tushery can vary in strength. It is not always as strong as in the following passage:

> Nay, but fair sir, now I bethink me, my Malkin abideth not the spur—Better it were that you tarry for the mare of our manciple down at the Grange, which may be had in little more than an an hour, and cannot but be tractable, in respect that she draweth much of our winter fire-wood, and eateth no corn.

Scott went to many places for his tushery. He got little precedent from the novel. Clara Reeve, Mrs Radcliffe, and M. G. Lewis use eighteenth-century English, more or less formal. Only Walpole in *The Castle of Otranto* gave him a lead. There we get such things as:

> "Villain! monster! sorcerer! 'tis thou hast done this! 'tis thou hast slain my son!"

and

> "Sir Knight, whoever thou art, I bid thee welcome. If thou art of mortal mould, thy valour shall meet its equal; and if thou art a true knight, thou wilt scorn to employ sorcery to carry thy point."

But the first passage is followed by one so little archaic as

"Think no more of him; he was a sickly puny child; and Heaven has perhaps taken him away, that I might not trust the honours of my house on so frail a foundation."

Walpole in fact rarely pushes his archaism beyond what was usual in the more solemn modes of eighteenth-century drama, in the historical plays, for instance, that Sheridan transfixed so neatly in *The Critic*: in this from Murphy's *Grecian Daughter*,

Philotas   By Heav'n thou wrong'st me: didst thou know, old man—
Melanthon   Could not his rev'rend age, could not his virtue, His woes unnumber'd, soften thee to pity?

or this from Thomas Francklin's *Earl of Warwick*,

Good Suffolk, lay aside
The forms of dull respect, be brief, and tell me.
Speak, hast thou seen her? Will she be my queen?
Quick, tell me ev'ry circumstance, each word,
Each look, each gesture: didst thou mark them, Suffolk?

or this from Richard Glover's *Boadicea*,

Why didst thou leave the fair Italian fields,
Thou silken slave of Venus? What could move
Thee to explore these boist'rous northern climes,
And change yon radiant sky for Britain's clouds?
What dost thou here, effeminate? By Heav'n,
Thou shouldst have loiter'd in Campania's villas,
And in thy garden nurs'd, with careful hands,
The gaudy-vested progeny of Flora.

If such mild archaising was behind the *Castle of Otranto* it may have been one of the miscellany of things behind *Ivanhoe* and much of the later Scott.

In the main, Scott went farther afield for his tushery. He had become acquainted at a very early age with archaic English through Percy's *Reliques*, and because of his prodigious memory these must have been a permanent part of his mind's furniture. He was soaked in Shakespeare and he was well versed in other Elizabethans. Berners's Froissart is another obvious source of the archaisms of *Ivanhoe*. We are apt to underestimate the extent and the boldness of Scott's archaising because we miss his originality in giving currency to many words or phrases that had dropped out. Ernest Weekley pointed this out in an article in the *Atlantic Monthly* for 1931 called *Walter Scott and the English Language*. Influenced by Percy and Shakespeare, Scott revived, among others, "passage of arms," "red-handed," "henchman," "stalwart." Very few readers of Scott are aware of such revivals: one of the reasons why they have taken his use of language so coolly.

When Scott archaised he did so with riotous eclecticism. It is a commonplace that his imitation of Euphuism through the mouth of Sir Piercie Shafton in the *Monastery* is most inaccurate; and naturally, for his exuberant mind was ill suited to the niggling accuracy required for successful pastiche. F. A. Pottle in his most interesting essay on the different types of memory in Boswell and Scott in *Essays on the Eighteenth Century*, presented to D. Nichol Smith, showed that Scott always added to what he remembered, being unable to suppress his creative urge: a process analogous to, or accounting for, his falsifying Lyly. So constituted, Scott would naturally draw on Chaucer, an old ballad, Froissart, and Shakespeare in the same paragraph as readily as Horace Walpole mixed his styles in the Gothic of Strawberry Hill. Indeed these words of Eastlake in his *History of the Gothic Revival* would apply *mutatis mutandis* to Scott's archaisms:

> The interior of Strawberry Hill was just what one might expect from a man who possessed a vague admiration for Gothic without the knowledge necessary for a proper adaptation of its features. Ceilings, screens, niches etc. are all copied, or rather parodied, from existing examples, but with utter disregard for the original purpose of the design. To Walpole Gothic was Gothic and that sufficed.

Add this tushery to the generally eighteenth-century ground of the language of *Ivanhoe* and you have something quite fantastically strange. It is Scott's triumph that he could be gloriously at ease in this strangeness and end by deceiving men into thinking he was doing something natural. Not that the triumph was not also a tragedy. In his attempt to cope with the English Middle Ages after coping with eighteenth-century Scotland Scott chose an instrument altogether coarser than the one he had discarded; and, though he showed a giant's strength in wielding it, nothing could alter the fact of its inferiority.

Scott tells us in the 1830 introduction to *Ivanhoe* that he chose an English subject for fear of cloying his readers with too much Scotland. In his next book, the *Monastery*, he reverted to Scotland but sought innovation by choosing a period intermediate between the eighteenth century and the reign of Richard I. But it appears from the turns and the inconsistences of the language he used that for about a third of the book he proceeded in uncertainty, hesitating between the manners of the Scottish novels and of *Ivanhoe*. In his first chapter, to be sure, describing the monastery of Kenna-quhair and its setting at the time of religious unrest in sixteenth-century Scotland he was sure of himself, because there is no dialogue and he can write in the language that was most natural to him. His troubles begin in the second chapter when after describing the tower of Glendearg and its inhabitants he embarks on a conversation between these and the English troopers who have been overrunning this part of the Lowlands. Elspeth Glendinning and her two sons belonged to a decent class of Scottish yeoman, and we know how Scott would have made them talk if he had followed his natural inclinations. All he allows Elspeth in the way of Scottish speech is a single *nae* for *no*; otherwise she talks English, as do her sons. When the kindly English captain, Stawarth Bolton, departs, Elspeth exclaims, "God be with you, gallant southern!", to which one boy retorts, "I will not say amen to a prayer for a southern," and the other, "Is it right to pray for a heretic?"; to which Elspeth replies:

The God to whom I pray only knows; but these two words, southern and heretic, have already cost Scotland ten thousand of her best and bravest, and me a husband, and you a father; and, whether blessing or banning, I never wish to hear them more.

What is remarkable in these speeches is that they are neither in the Scots that such characters would have used in the Scottish novels nor in the tushery they would probably have used in *Ivanhoe*.

The scene now changes to the castle of Lady Avenel, widow of Walter Avenel, a Baron of ancient descent. Hearing that the tower of Glendearg has been spared by the English marauders, she decides to take refuge there to escape the dangers that threaten her castle. She is accompanied in her flight by her shepherd and his wife. When Martin and Tibb Tacket open their mouths, Scott, in spite of his treatment of the Glendinnings' speech, allows them to break into the Scots of which he was the supreme master. There follow the best things in this very unsatisfactory novel: the flight of Lady Avenel with her infant daughter and the two Tackets across the moor, their kind reception by Elspeth Glendinning, and the subsequent life of the combined households, These are in Scott's cleanest and most delicate domestic vein: the minute frictions set up by the different social positions of the two families and the compromises by which they are overcome are recounted or hinted at with the skill of a great master. And Elspeth Glendinning, oblivious of her previous speech, talks the Scots that she should of course have talked from the beginning:

> "And what made you, ye misleard loons," said Dame Elspeth to her two boys, "come yon gate into the ha', roaring like bull-segs, to frighten the leddy, and her far frae strong? Could ye find nae night for daffin but Hallowe'en, and nae time but when the leddy was reading to us about the holy Saints? May ne'er be in my fingers, if I dinna sort ye baith for it!"

When the scene changes to the monastery, Scott has to decide what language his monks are to use; and, in spite of the success of what has just gone before, he makes these sixteenth-century Scottish monks talk much like their brethren in the late twelfth-century setting of *Ivanhoe*. Here is part of the first conversation; between the Abbot and his Sacristan.

"The lady is unwell, holy father," answered the Sacristan, "and unable to bear the journey."

"True—ay—yes—then must one of our brethren go to her—Knowest thou if she hath aught of a jointure from this Walter de Avenel?"

"Very little, holy father," answered the Sacristan, "she hath resided at Glendearg since her husband's death, wellnigh on the charity of a poor widow, called Elspeth Glendinning.

"Why, thou knowest all the widows in the countryside?" said the Abbot. "Ho! ho! ho!" and he shook his portly sides at his own jest.

Unsettled by his decision on the speech of the Scottish monks, Scott goes back on his other decision to make Elspeth Glendinning talk in the Scots that becomes her, for, when the Sacristan comes to Glendearg and talks with her about the sick lady, all the Scots she can attain to is an occasional *nae doubt*, and the pattern of her talk is this kind of thing:

And yet is the Holy Scripture communicated for our common salvation. Good father, you must instruct mine ignorance better; but lack of wit cannot be a deadly sin, and truly, to my poor thinking, I should be glad to read the Holy Scriptures.

From now till near half way the queerest linguistic confusion reigns. For instance, in the eighth chapter Elspeth talks English for a long stretch, breaks into a bit of Scots, reverts to English, and then resumes her Scots for a moment. A humble character, Peter the Bridgeward, speaks tushery: "By my sooth, sir, you look sorely travelled and deadly pale." When Halbert Glendinning encounters the ghostly White Lady, both description and dialogue are in the pure idiom of the Neo-Gothic romance:

"Speak!" he said, wildly tossing his arms, "speak yet again—be once more present, lovely vision!—thrice have I now seen thee, yet the idea of thy invisible presence around or beside me, makes my heart beat faster than if the earth yawned and gave up a demon."

Not only Elspeth switches from English to Scots and back

again, but so does the homely Hob Miller. Unlike Elspeth's, his English is mainly tushery ("And so I say, dame, an ye be so busied with your housewife-skep, or aught else . . .") while his Scots is perfunctory. Into the existing linguistic chaos breaks Sir Piercie Shafton with his pseudo-Euphuism. The final degradation is when Martin the shepherd, who had been the occasion of Scott's changing to the idiom proper to such characters, uses the colourless language of the inferior romantic novels of the late eighteenth century:

> God help me, there may be truth in what thou sayest—but walk slower, for my old limbs cannot keep pace with your young legs— walk slower, and I will tell you why age, though unlovely, is yet endurable.

After this lapse Scott begins to settle into what was to be the linguistic norm of most of his later novels. There are a few returns to Scots but one hardly notices them; and when Halbert gets out into the wider world to seek his fortunes, the linguistic tone is the historico-heroic one, full energetic unsubtle, that began with *Ivanhoe* and that was to serve Scott's turn so usefully in his later popular successes. In the scenes in Avenel Castle with Julian Avenel, his timid mistress, Henry Warden the Protestant preacher, and Halbert Glendinning, we feel that Scott at last knows his own mind; his energies, though coarsened, are unimpeded. In the *Abbot* he maintained the temper he had reached in the course of the *Monastery*. There may be a dozen bits of Scots in the whole book, but for all its Scottish setting it is linguistically in full harmony with its successor, set in England, *Kenilworth*.

Thereafter Scott was occasionally tempted to return to his earliest manner, but a Scottish setting was not in itself sufficient to give the incentive. The *Fair Maid of Perth* maintains the historico-heroic norm, and we get in it a thing like, "Nay, God-a-mercy, wench, it were hard to deny thee time to busk thy body-clothes." It was only when Scott felt the paramount urge to work his remaining Jacobitism out of his system that he consented to resume his old linguistic habits in *Redgauntlet*. Twice he made a partial return: first, and in a more important way, in the *Pirate*; second in the

Fortunes of Nigel. In the *Pirate* Scott returns for a little to his true domestic vein in describing the households of Jarlshof and Stourburgh, but in the end melodrama prevails. In the *Fortunes of Nigel* there are no complete circles where the Scottish idiom is used and the tushery is especially strong:

> O! Saint Dunstan has caught his eye; pray God he swallow not the images. See how he stands astonished, as old Adam and Eve ply their Ding-dong! Come, Frank, thou art a scholar; construe me that same fellow, with his blue cap with a cock's feather in it, to show he's of gentle blood, God wot.

But while the hero, Nigel Olifaunt, speaks English, against all probability as fresh from Scotland, his servant, Richie Moniplies, speaks Scots consistently. The other character who speaks Scots is the king himself; Scott, I take it, feeling unable to be quite false to James's written words. But it sounds queer when he talks thus, while one of his Scots nobles speaks an English of which the following is a sample:

> It is a lie, a false lie, forge it who list!—It is true I wore a dagger of service by my side, and not a bodkin like yours, to pick one's teeth withal—and for prompt service—Odds nouns! it should be prompt to be useful.

In neither novel are there the turns and contradictions that make the *Monastery* so strangely unstable for near half of its course.

Scott's linguistic vagaries are matched by his states of mind. Generalisations, like those of Bagehot, about the way Scott always views his material from without are false. When in his early Scottish novels he felt free to use the speech that came most naturally to him he can be (I do not say always was) as close to his scenes and characters as Jane Austen. But in response to the public demand he abandoned the intimacy he had loved and turned his prodigious vitality to pageantry and stirring improbabilities. For these ends he created a strange linguistic amalgam, an amalgam that suited his readers so well that they overlooked its strangeness. The *Monastery* is uniquely interesting as showing the conflict between Scott's two modes in the very act of being resolved.

Shelley's "Ozymandias"

I met a traveller from an antique land
Who said: Two vast and trunkless legs of stone
Stand in the desert. . . . Near them, on the sand,
Half sunk, a shattered visage lies, whose frown,
And wrinkled lip, and sneer of cold command,
Tell that its sculptor well those passions read
Which yet survive, stamped on these lifeless things,
The hand that mocked them, and the heart that fed:
And on the pedestal these words appear:
'My name is Ozymandias, king of kings:
Look on my works, ye Mighty, and despair!'
Nothing beside remains. Round the decay
Of that colossal wreck, boundless and bare,
The lone and level sands stretch far away.

I HAVE been astonished to find how many readers go astray over the bare sense of this sonnet; and readers who imagine that Shelley had a muddled mind and was at any time capable of nonsense are especially prone to such aberration. One confusion was over the relations of the man who made the statue and the man the statue represented. One reader at least has been known to think that Ozymandias was the sculptor and that the words on the pedestal were his, addressed in the first instance to his patron ("king of kings") and in the second to his fellow-sculptors ("ye Mighty"). His works would be the statue in question and others from his chisel in the vicinity; and his rivals are asked to despair because he has secured such good contracts among the aristocracy.

But the worst trouble came in the middle with the lines,

Tell that its sculptor well those passions read
Which yet survive, stamped on these lifeless things,
The hand that mocked them, and the heart that fed.

Several readers, to my knowledge, took *stamped* as an active preterite having *passions* as subject and *hand* and *heart* as objects. The passions first survived and then stamped a hand and a heart on *those lifeless things*, which could only be the trunkless legs and the shattered visage. The mix-up of anatomy was so appalling that the only conclusion was that Shelley (as usual) was mad.

Such being some of the possible aberrations, let me give the sonnet's plain sense: In the desert lie the remains—two legs and a head—of a colossal statue of an Egyptian king called Ozymandias. The face preserves the cynical and the tyrannical passions that animated the king. But the sculptor in making the portrait knew his model and brought out those qualities in a satirical spirit. These passions and the sculptor's shrewd and satirical sense of them have outlasted, through the preservation of the fragments, both the hand of the sculptor who mockingly made the statue and the king out of whose heart the passions sprang. The words on the pedestal belong to Ozymandias and show that round about the statue stood all the works—temples, basilicas, statues—he had caused to be set up. These were so many and so large that other mighty kings are bidden despair of competing. Now, nothing remains of all these works but the fragments of his own shattered image. And around lies nothing but desert.

You may complain that I have omitted a part of the sense: namely the traveller from an antique land who gives the information in the first line and one-fifth of the second. I did so deliberately, for the traveller does not belong to the *sense* at all. He is pure machinery; and his function is to make us ready to accept the startling, abrupt description of the statue. And he succeeds; for we all *expect* a surprise in a traveller's tale. Shelley manipulates our expectations with the greatest skill and with a speed that simply could not be bettered. The speed is also a warrant for the intensity of Shelley's feeling, which leads to the next question: what is the nature of that feeling?

He does not keep us waiting long, for it appears in the third line through the posture of the vast legs. As far as the *sense* goes, they could have lain: thus disposed they would have given equally good archaeological evidence of the size and nature of the statue. By making them stand trunkless in the desert the poet turns them to ridicule: they are doing no job through their position; they are a mere superfluous erection. Whether their ludicrousness is pathetic, calling for pity, or merited, calling for scorn, we do not yet know. The poet does not leave us long in doubt. From his account of the battered face we gather at once that he feels hatred and derision. The word *visage* is intentionally and successfully pompous, suggesting size and (in the context) overbearingness in its owner. *Sneer of cold command*, plainly hostile, confirms the impression. Indeed I find that it overdoes the confirmation. Here (and here only and only for a moment) Shelley's private political resentments, his revolutionary hatred of priests and kings, peep out. In a poem where elsewhere the language is natural, unadorned, but fresh and (shall I call it?) genuinely desired, the phrase *sneer of cold command* peeps out banal and melodramatic, vaguely emotive instead of precisely felt, a flicker of propagandist zeal.

But Shelley recovers and gives us his first pregnant equivocation. What does he mean by the passions' surviving? In a prose sense he need mean no more than that the personal passions of Ozymandias have survived through the chance preservation of the statue's face. But the grandeur of the lines (which show Shelley's characteristic power of ennobling simple words) suggest that general truths emerge from the specific detail. These may be: that lifeless stone can survive living dynasties; that the passions, the general human feelings, survive the individual and persist through the ages; perhaps even that they are our problem now, as they were then, that we have our own Ozymandiases to reckon with; and, last, the truism that life is short and art long.

The climax comes with a piece of irony. When Ozymandias tells the mighty to look on his work and despair he meant their motive of desperation to be their inability to build so solidly and so vastly as himself. But his words became true in another sense. His works have perished, and the mighty of the world may despair of ever erecting anything to resist the consuming force of time. Even the most arrogant assertion of the human spirit in the most massive material is ludicrously weak. Thus Ozymandias, thinking he says one thing, actually says another.

The last three lines,

> Nothing beside remains. Round the decay
> Of that colossal wreck, boundless and bare,
> The lone and level sands stretch far away,

are powerful in feeling and much more than mere descriptive setting. The three simple words *nothing beside remains*, three measured dissyllables, fall coldly and critically after the great king's resounding protestation: they are perfectly calculated to deflate pomp. The rest has been criticised for redundance, *bare* and *lone* on the one hand, and *boundless* and *far away* on the other, being too reduplicatory. But *bare* and *lone* are not redundant. *Bare* means "devoid of vegetation"; *lone*, "devoid of human beings." *Boundless* and *far away* certainly overlap in their primary senses. But a good deal of poetry (some of Shakespeare's sonnets for instance) says the same things in different ways and with different degrees of emphasis. Here, *boundless* states the idea, while the open vowels of *far away* suggest the physical expanse of the sands. Thus there is no emotional redundance. On the contrary, Shelley amplifies in order to convey a new element of emotion. This novelty is achieved partly by the way he manipulates the sonnet form. The Petrarchian sonnet, of which *Ozymandias* is an example, contains two self-contained metrical units: one of eight lines with a self-complete set of interlocked rhymes, followed by another of six with a set of different rhymes. And usually the sentiments expressed in octave and sestet are different, often contrasted. Shelley breaks the custom by continuing the sentiment of the octave into half of the sestet, ending it with the eleventh line and leaving only three lines to introduce his new sentiment or to point his contrast. The result is twofold. By giving so much room to Ozymandias Shelley heightens the sense of the man's grasping pride. By reducing the counter-statement to three lines he implies that it must be surpassingly powerful to need so little space, thereby hinting at the nature of the power that confronts the great king's assertions. The novelty of these last three lines is that in them Shelley's feeling for the metaphysical has revealed itself. The desert has become a symbol; it is the same as the "deserts of vast eternity" in Marvell's *To his Coy Mistress*. It is in these that the tyrant's passions look so petty. The ultimate effect of the sonnet is thus, in undogmatic sense, religious. And the religion is the more emphatic because there is no statement of it; it arises from the conclusions we unconsciously draw from the poem's formal features.

I have mentioned Marvell's *Coy Mistress*; but for an apter general analogy with Shelley's sonnet I think of Isabella's speech in *Measure for Measure* on tyrants, on men clothed with a little brief authority, playing apelike such fantastic tricks before high heaven as make the angels weep. The passion here is close to Shelley's. On the other hand Shakespeare's "high heaven" is less rarefied than Shelley's metaphysical desert. As well as feeling vehemently against tyrants Shelley could, within the compass of fourteen lines, distance them, producing a sentiment not unlike Thomas Browne's in his exclamations in *Urn Burial* at the futility of seeking perpetual fame:

> Others, rather than be lost in the uncomfortable night of Nothing, were content to recede into the common Being, and make one particle of the public soul of all things, which was no more than to return into their unknown and divine original again. Egyptian ingenuity was more unsatisfied, contriving their bodies in sweet consistences to attend the return of their souls. But all was vanity, feeding the wind, and folly. The Egyptian mummies, which Cambyses or time hath spared, avarice now consumeth. Mummy is become merchandise, Mizrain cures wounds, and Pharoah is sold for balsams. In vain do individuals hope for immortality or any patent from oblivion, in preservations below the moon.

But if Browne resembles Shelley in seeing things from a distance, he differs from him through his ingenuity. Between the two men there had intervened the eighteenth century. There is in Shelley's sonnet a luminousness, a directness, an absence of fuss or qualification unlike anything in Browne.

That luminousness has to do partly with the style, a style that retained the lucidity of the Augustan age while rejecting its conventional personifications and antitheses. But Shelley had reasons for using the current modifications of the eighteenth-century idiom that constituted the Romantic idiom in an especially assured and hence luminous way. He was the son of an eighteenth-century aristocrat, and for all his vagaries of thought, he retained a singleness of mind and an assurance in keeping with his origin. Whatever Shelley wrote was his own, but in this sonnet as well as elsewhere he revealed his debt to the people among whom he was bred. It was partly on this account that, when he wrote at his height, Shelley mastered the simple sublime as no English poet since him has ever been able to do.

Thomas Love Peacock

An open lecture on an author like Peacock calls for a technique different from one suited to Shakespeare or Milton. Peacock is relished by a small number of readers; and in a general audience you could count on only a small percentage of Peacockians. Part will scarcely know him at all; another part may know him from one or two rousing lyrics, like the *War-song of Dinas Vawr*:

> The mountain sheep are sweeter,
> But the valley sheep are fatter;
> We therefore deemed it meeter
> To carry off the latter;

another part may have supplemented their interest in Shelley's *Defence of Poetry* by reading Peacock's *Four Ages of Poetry*, which it provoked; only a minority will have read the works of Peacock that make him the unique figure he is, the novels. The lecturer then will find himself as much in the position of propagandist as of explicator or critic. And if he wants to fulfil his function as the first, if he wants to persuade people that by not reading Peacock's novels they are missing something rich and rare, he will have to go gently with them, taking little for granted, and telling them the kind of fact about the man it would be ridiculous to tell about Shakespeare or Milton. If in lecturing on these two authors I informed you that Shakespeare left his second best bed to his wife or that Milton went blind in middle age, I cannot believe you would thank me. On the other hand, if I plunged straight into a criticism of *Melincourt* or *Gryll Grange*, on the assumption that you all had these works well in the front of your minds at this present moment, I cannot believe you would thank me either. So I will attempt the best middle course I can devise and say something about Peacock, man and author, generally, before going on to the novels themselves.

Thomas Love Peacock was a satirist, not the greatest of English satirists but one of the most charming and most amiable. Unlike some others (Swift and the author of *Hudibras* for instance) he tempers satire with kindliness, wit with humour, cynicism with romance, the scorn of society with a belief in the domestic virtues. And he adds a dash of gay, outrageous, and quite un-cruel farce (again unlike the author of *Hudibras*) that makes one think less of the satirists proper than of the comic writers, Chaucer among the English and Aristophanes among the Greeks.

Peacock was born in 1785, the year in which De Quincey too was born, being younger than Wordsworth, Scott, and Coleridge, and older than Shelley and Keats. He is thus right in the middle of the Romantic Revival period; and yet he belonged to no group within it. He got to know Shelley by accident, and the two became friends; but they were anything but partners in creation. Nor could Peacock have partnered anyone. The whole point of his writing is its detachment, its freedom to change sides. If he had joined a movement with a creed and a programme he would have killed the type of creativeness he commanded. On the other hand he is the herald, if not the ancestor, of later men with the same gift of the athletic *volte-face*: Samuel Butler of *Erewhon* and George Bernard Shaw. Shaw's glorification of royalism and his guying of socialist politicians in the *Apple Cart*, after the things he had said on the other side, would have been after Peacock's heart.

Peacock would have been an isolated author, an onlooker not a co-operator, whatever his circumstances; but these did in fact confirm what was a natural bent. His father, a glass-merchant, died when he was young; he was an only child; and his upbringing was in the hands of his mother, helped partly by his maternal grandfather, an old sea-captain who had lost a leg in a naval engagement. Mrs Peacock was well educated and bookish and passed on her tastes to her son. Between seven and thirteen he was at boarding-school near Windsor Park; and that was all the regular schooling he had. Those were the days before compulsory games became part of boarding-school life (Lytton Strachey describes them in his essay on Thomas Arnold in *Eminent Victorians*), and Peacock was free to acquire the habit, and then to indulge the passion, of long walks and explorations in the country. The more common process of having corners rubbed off at a large school and having them rubbed on again at college did not apply to Peacock. He learned to read for himself and to find his own way in the country; and those two lessons he continued to make use of for a great part of his life. They are two lessons that go together remarkably well. Things read have to be digested if they are to nourish; and one of the best digestives so far discovered is exercise in the open, not too violent and not too exciting.

Peacock ranged wide in his reading. What he *liked* best was Greek and Italian poetry; and those tastes are evident in his novels. But he did not avoid the writings that formed the thought of his own day. Indeed it is these and the politics of his time that provide the material for his satire as well as the nourishment of his thought. He had read Rousseau and temperamentally he was very greatly drawn to Rousseauish theories of the educative value of solitude in nature and of the innate virtue of uncorrupted man. And yet he was not in the least danger of swallowing Rousseau whole. Even when he shows himself most in sympathy, good sense and the coolness of unillusioned criticism insist on intruding. One of the most delightful and indeed one of the most romantic chapters in Peacock's novels is the fourteenth of *Crotchet Castle*, entitled *The Dingle*. It describes the meeting, in the mountains of Wales, of the hero, Mr Chainmail, and the heroine, Miss Susannah Touchandgo; and I fancy it lies behind two notable descriptions in the novels of his son-in-law George Meredith, the meeting of Richard and Lucy in the *Ordeal of Richard Feverel* and of Clara Middleton's coming on Vernon Whitford asleep under the wild cherry-tree in the *Egoist*. Miss Touchandgo, reduced from wealth to a modest way of life through the bankruptcy and absconding of her speculative father, has gone to live in a simple farmhouse in Wales and receives the impression of the grand mountain scenery that surrounds her. It is with no jot of satire that Peacock heads his chapter with a quotation from Wordsworth:

The stars of midnight shall be dear
To her, and she shall lean her ear
    In many a secret place,
Where rivulets dance their wayward round;
And beauty, born of murmuring sound,
    Shall pass into her face.

But when he describes in detail, at the beginning of the chapter, the influence of Rousseau on the heroine, it is not long before good sense and the critical spirit mingle themselves with romance:

Miss Susannah Touchandgo had read the four great poets of Italy, and many of the best writers of France. About the time of her father's downfall, accident threw into her way *Les Rêveries du Promeneur Solitaire;* and from the impression which these made on her, she carried with her into retirement all the works of Rousseau. In the midst of that startling light which the conduct of old friends, on a sudden reverse of fortune, throws on a young and inexperienced mind, the doctrines of the philosopher of Geneva struck with double force upon her sympathies: she imbibed the sweet poison, as somebody calls it, of his writings even to a love of truth; which, every wise man knows, ought to be left to those who can get anything by it. The society of children, the beauties of nature, the solitude of the montains, became her consolation, and, by degrees, her delight. The gay society from which she had been excluded remained on her memory only as a disagreeable dream. She imbibed her new monitor's ideas of simplicity of dress, assimilating her own with that of the peasant girls in the neighbourhood; the black hat, the blue gown, the black stockings, the shoes tied on the instep.

It is true that she somewhat modified the forms of her rustic dress; to the black hat she added a black feather, to the blue gown she added a tippet and a waistband fastened in front with a silver buckle; she wore her black stockings very smooth and tight on her ankles, and tied her shoes in tasteful bows with the nicest possible ribbon. In this apparel, to which, in winter, she added a scarlet cloak, she made dreadful havoc among the rustic mountaineers.

Peacock quite genuinely   believes that the doctrines of

Rousseau and of Wordsworth after all have their effect and should do so: but he knows that this effect can go only a certain way and he thinks that to pretend it goes farther is to be blind or a knave. But the intrusion of the critical spirit in this passage does not prevent Peacock going on to describe in all sincerity the pool and waterfall that were Susannah's favourite haunt and the unaffected feelings she brought to it and drew from it.

Peacock had read the works of Turgot and Condorcet advancing the doctrine of human progress and the retort that Malthus in his *Essay on Population* regretfully made in assertion of its impossiblity. The kind of use to which Peacock put his reading can be seen in his *Four Ages of Poetry*, which is a kind of parody of Condorcet's *Esquisse des Progrès de l'Esprit humain*, a book presenting a series of historical tableaux, showing pictures of the world's improvement. Peacock, adopting ironically Condorcet's general thesis, argues that literature has flourished not directly but inversely with the rise of civilisation. While Homer's age was barbarous, Homer himself was the supreme poet. While the present age has made unexampled progress in science, its poets are narrow and conceited. Buoyed up by a limited success in exploiting the picturesque, they have had their heads turned, "mistaking the prominent novelty for the all-important totality"; and Peacock puts into their mouths the theories they profess to be acting on; he imagines these poets saying:

"Poetical genius is the finest of all things, and we feel that we have more of it than any one ever had. The way to bring it to perfection is to cultivate poetical impressions exclusively. Poetical impressions can be received only among natural scenes, for all that is artificial is anti-poetical. Society is artificial, therefore we will live out of society. The mountains are natural, therefore we will live in the mountains. There we shall be shining models of purity and virtue, passing the whole day in the innocent and amiable occupation of going up and down hill, receiving poetical impressions, and communicating them in immortal verse to admiring generations."

Poetry, Peacock says, is thus in its dotage and will soon give way to the more serious concerns of humanity. And as instances of those more serious concerns he describes the various modern triumphs in technology and economics that are the usual target for his satire. You need not take Peacock's adaptation of Condorcet too seriously. He adopts a position, not because he believes in it but because it is a useful vantage-point from which to attack a piece of pretentiousness. Nevertheless, you *can* be certain that he is always on the side of a proper sense of proportion and of the sanctity of the fundamental human feelings.

I mentioned the Welsh sitting in *Crotchet Castle*; and his first vist to Wales, in 1810, was to have marked effect on his life as well as on the substance of some of his novels. It was in Wales that he met the woman he was to marry, and the one friend he was to have among the major literary men of his age, Shelley. It was a friendship that does credit to both, for without mutual tolerance two such hopelessly different people must have flown apart or quarrelled. Shelley had a religious and mystical temperament, however unorthodox the forms it took; Peacock had little religious sense and an eye that detected the least tendency to extravagance. But they shared two passions, the love of natural scenery and the love of Greek literature, which were enough to bring them together initially and to allow that strong, illogical, mutual liking that is the basis of all true friendship to do its work. Peacock, though a satirist and a cynic, was perfectly willing to bear with the extravagancy of Shelley's enthusiasms if he was allowed to laugh at them; and, happening to prize honesty and absence of affectation above most things, could not miss them in his friend. Shelley on his side was affectionate and well disposed to anyone who did not think of him as a monster of wickedness and infidelity and must soon have learnt to appreciate the qualities of kindliness and honesty that were so strong in Peacock. About the time Peacock and Shelley met, the Shelleys had got mixed up in a society of well-intentioned but superficial folk who shared his views about how the world ought to be reformed. It is a kind of society that is constantly with us; in England it finds a particularly congenial setting in the so-called Garden Cities or Garden Suburbs. Peacock in his *Memoirs of Shelley* gives his experience of it:

> At Bracknell, Shelley was surrounded by a numerous society, all in a great measure of his own opinions in relation to religion and politics, and the larger portion of them in relation to vegetable diet. But they wore their rue with a difference. Everyone of them, adopting some of the articles of the faith of their general church, had each nevertheless some predominant crotchet of his or her own, which left a number of open questions for earnest and not always temperate discussion. I was sometimes irreverent enough to laugh at the fervour with which opinions utterly unconducive to any practical result were battled for as matters of the highest importance to the well-being of mankind; Harriet Shelley was always ready to laugh with me, and we thereby both lost caste with some of the more hot-hearted of the party.

Naturally these enthusiasts looked on Peacock as an alien and thought that Shelley was bound to cast him off. They were wrong on both counts. Peacock enjoyed the society he laughed at, while Shelley found in Peacock the most loyal and trustworthy and durable of all his friends.

Shelley and Peacock owed much to each other. Peacock recognised and strengthened the force and the toughness that underlay Shelley's silly habits and strange mental aberrations, a force which would have become more and more evident if Shelley had lived longer. On the other side I believe it was no accident that Peacock's close intercourse with Shelley coincided with his first effective writing. Contact with a man of superior genius gave Peacock's mind an extra dose of astringent energy that pulled the scattered contents of that mind together and gave them artistic form. Hence his first novel, *Headlong Hall*, which began the series on which his reputation as man of letters rests. The character Scythrop in *Nightmare Abbey*, vacillating between two young women, is a travesty of Shelley vacillating between Harriet and Mary Godwin. Peacock never put the whole of a character from life into a single character in one of his novels; he chooses no more than a single side. And if Scythrop is based on a small portion of Shelley, the virtuous Mr Forester in *Melincourt*, who has ideals and, surprisingly, lives up to them, is based on another side. The Hon. Mrs Pinmoney, seeing him for the first time, asks, "Who is that very bright-eyed wild-looking young man?", a description that applies to Shelley very closely. But the following reminiscence of one of Shelley's poems shows a deeper debt; and all the deeper for being probably unconscious.

One of the most exciting and at the same time most amusing incidents in Peacock's second novel, *Melincourt*, is that of the heroine, Anthelia, on one of her solitary walks in the Lake District mountains, surprised by a storm on an island-rock in a torrent, cut off, and finally rescued by Sir Oran Haut-ton, the chivalrous and well-dressed orang-outang, caught very young in the forests of Angola, carefully civilised, furnished with a purchased baronetcy, and destined to become one of the two members of Parliament for the rotten borough of Onevote. The description of the landscape and of the torrent is clearly animated by the descriptions of scenery in Shelley's *Alastor*, written not long before, whose very name was due to a suggestion of Peacock's; Anthelia, of course, in her solitary roaming, corresponding to Shelley's poetic hero in *Alastor*. The resemblance is strongest with the end of *Alastor*, describing the poet's final resting-place in a nook by a stream shooting over a chasm. There is a solitary pine-tree extending over the chasm, and the resting-place is full of autumnal leaves. Correspondingly there is in *Melincourt* a "romantic chasm" (*Melincourt* was published not long after *Kubla Khan*), with a torrent, a bridge, a solitary tree, and autumnal leaves. This is how Peacock describes the place before the storm breaks:

> Anthelia descended through a grove of pines into a romantic chasm, where a foaming stream was crossed by a rude and ancient bridge, consisting of two distinct parts, each of which rested against a columnar rock, that formed an island in the roaring waters. An ash had fixed its roots in the fissures of the rock, and the knotted base of its aged trunk offered to the passenger a natural seat, overcanopied with its beautiful branches, and leaves now

tinged with their autumnal yellow. Anthelia rested awhile in this delightful solitude. There was no breath of wind, no song of birds, no humming of insects, only the dashing of the waters beneath. She felt the presence of the genius of the scene.

Later, there is a cloud-burst. An oak-tree, carried down by the torrent, breaks up one of the bridges connecting rock and valley-side. But Anthelia watches the swollen waters, fascinated, and not perceiving that they are in the act of undermining the foundation of the other bridge. Peacock goes on:

> She was roused from her reverie only by the sound of the bridge's dissolution. She looked back, and found herself on the solitary rock insulated by the swelling flood. Would the flood rise above the level of the rock? The ash must in that case be her refuge. Could the force of the torrent rend its massy roots from the rocky fissures which grasped them with giant strength? Nothing could seem less likely: yet it was not impossible. But she had always looked with calmness on the course of necessity: she felt that she was always in the order of nature. Though her life had been a series of uniform prosperity, she had considered deeply the changes of things and "the nearness of the paths of night and day" in every pursuit and circumstance of human life. She sat on the stem of the ash. The torrent rolled almost at her feet. Could this be the calm sweet scene of the morning, the ivied bridges, the romantic chasm, the stream far below, bright in its bed of rocks, chequered by the pale sunbeams through the leaves of the ash?

I cannot believe that Peacock would have allowed himself that solemnity about Anthelia's thoughts in her danger but for the influence of Shelley. But the solemn mood passes quickly, for Sir Oran Haut-ton, who happens to be in the neighbourhood, sees her plight, deliberately uproots a pine-tree with all the native strength of the orang-outang, makes an extemporary bridge with it, crosses over, and proceeds to carry Anthelia back to safety. The grotesqueness following the solemnity restores the true Peacockian balance. Though swayed by Shelley, Peacock was not persuaded by him against his true instincts.

After two or three years of close friendship, the ways of

Shelley and Peacock parted. Shelley left England, never to return; Peacock obtained a regular and responsible post in the office of the East India Company. He was a most efficient civil servant, thus adding one more piece of testimony to the generally overlooked truth that most creative artists are perfectly competent practical men if they choose to set their minds to practical things. When they are incompetent it is because they will not be bothered, not because they lack the ability. Committed to the practical life, Peacock was forced to compromise on matters of principle. He was one of the earliest sceptics concerning the benefits of material progress. Long before Ruskin he questioned the use of being able to travel more quickly between two places if the two places were in themselves undesirable. So it is a delightful irony, of a perfectly Peacockian kind, that one of his duties at the East India office was to improve communications between India and Great Britain. He carried it out with conspicuous success, being the originator of a rapid steamship service between the countries. And, in spite of his principles, he could not refrain from talking affectionately of what he called his "iron chickens." He survived along with Landor well into the Victorian age, a relic of a generation so large a proportion of whose writers of genius died young. His composition of his last novel, *Gryll Grange*, in 1860, is one not only of the delights but of the curiosities of literature.

In his book on comedy L. J. Potts sites Peacock's novels on the borderline between comedy and satire: "perhaps in a no-man's land." And this admission of an admixture of comedy will serve to correct what I think is a mistaken general statement in Carl Van Doren's excellent biography. In commenting on a certain seriousness and didacticism in *Melincourt* he writes:

> Peacock seems not yet to have been willing to pay the cynic's penalty of laughing at what he secretly admired, sustained by the consciousness that in the cynic branch of comedy all things are folly, in a sense, and fit for nothing so much as laughter.

It is not true that for the developed Peacock *all* things are
fit for nothing so much as laughter. In fact, the very unique-
ness of Peacock and his prime virtue is that in the very
act of laughing he gives the assurance that he has certain
beliefs and allegiances. Mrs Campbell is right when she
says:

> Impartial mockery is never funny for very long, from sheer lack
> of contrast, and because the finest humour depends on a distinct
> *partiality* for human nature; and on a half-rueful sense of the
> pitifulness as well as the comicality of its efforts to be effective and
> wise.

Now what approximates Peacock to comedy and underlies
and tempers his satire is the strength of his own affections
and his belief in the human affections generally. Whatever he
mocks at it is never these. In life he tempered an inflexible
refusal to yield his opinions to any man, with a strong social
sense. He was ever willing to serve his friends, though ever
unwilling to accommodate his opinions to theirs. And it is
opinions, the progeny of the heated brain, he satirises, never
the fundamental pieties and affections that bind men together in societies. Now, since man in society is the sphere of
comedy, it is evident that Peacock's variegated satire is
united with a fundamentally comic spirit.

I pass now to the individual novels. There are seven of
them. Of these, five are constructed on one pattern. The
setting is that of English or Welsh country houses, where a
number of guests typifying each some particular opinion or
crank (*humorous* characters in Ben Jonson's sense) meet
together, harangue, argue, make love, have grotesque adventures, and get married. These five novels are all short, with
Melincourt less short than the rest. Elegance and brevity are
necessary to prevent so artificial creations from becoming
tedious. All these short novels succeed, but I put *Crotchet
Castle* as the best of them all. The other two, *Maid Marion*
and the *Misfortunes of Elphin* are mock-historical, the first
concerning the Robin Hood legends of the English Middle
Ages, the second sixth-century Wales. In these there is less
talk and more plot; but the same virtues of elegance and

brevity are present. Peacock delights in satirising the sentimental and heroic accounts of the past by introducing the
realistically homely, the topical, and the absurd. It is a
method that goes back to Euripides in his *Electra*. In this play
Euripides gives his version of the Electra story as it really
might have happened today if it were true, thereby satirising
the heroic versions current till his time. Peacock is less grim
and more grotesque; and for a rather closer comparison we
can go to Bernard Shaw's *Caesar and Cleopatra*. But Peacock's mixture of elegance, romance, satire, and farce is all
his own; and these two pseudo-historical novelettes have
their unique, and to me highly attractive, flavour.

Peacock's brevity and tact come out not only in the total
length of his novels but in the length of his scenes. Like
Jane Austen's his technique is nearer to drama than to
narrative; and the dialogue groups itself into units resembling scenes from a play. It is of a playwright's work that
Peacock's novels sometimes remind me. The plays of Lyly,
although two hundred and fifty-odd years earlier, have the
same kind of brevity, sophistication, and charm. They also
stand somewhat aside from the great Elizabethan drama as
Peacock does from his greater contemporaries. Another
resemblance is in the young women. Lyly's Campaspe is
slightly drawn yet she combines health and charm much in
the way most of Peacock's heroines do.

The brevity and tact have the further use of civilising the
satire. For the satire is broad, the characters are mere embodiments of single humours and would soon bore if they
talked for too long. Not being bitter and on the whole liking
his fellow-men Peacock avoids the extremes of the older
Samuel Butler and of Swift. *Hudibras* is violent and bitter
against a whole section of its author's compatriots; it is vain
to deny the pathological element in Swift's detestation of
mankind. Peacock forgets the man in the "humour" and,
through forgetting, forgives. Nevertheless he is sharply
conscious of the dominance of selfish motives in human
conduct. Not that he is not resigned to seeing these govern a
large proportion of men's acts. It is when grand names are
given to selfish deeds that he is moved to protest. At the

beginning of the *Misfortunes of Elphin* there is an account of the port of Gwythno in Wales:

> This port, we may believe if we please, had not been unknown to the Phoenicians and Carthaginians, when they visited the island for metal, accommodating the inhabitants, in return, with luxuries which they would not otherwise have dreamed of and which they could very well have done without; of course, in arranging the exchange of what they denominated equivalents, imposing on their simplicity and taking advantage of their ignorance, according to the approved practice of civilized nations; which they called imparting the blessings of Phoenician and Carthaginian light.

There is similar satire on the discrepancy between men's principles and their conduct. Peacock puts up with, and is amused by, their conduct, but he must protest and laugh at the silly way in which they humbug themselves that they are acting up to principles which in fact they cannot genuinely hold. Mr Chainmail, in *Crotchet Castle*, has made up his mind on principle that he will not marry a lady whose ancestry cannot be traced back to the Middle Ages, yet he fails to resist the charm of the pedigreeless Miss Touchandgo. Dr Gaster in *Headlong Hall* rejoices "that the antediluvian patriarchs knew not the use of the grape" and laps up a bumper of Burgundy. Mr Escott, the deteriationist, sitting out at a ball (while the beautiful Miss Cranium is dancing with someone else), contrasts the splendid natural dances of the American Indian with modern ball-room decadence but rushes off a moment after to dance with Miss Cranium

> and probably felt at least as happy among the chandeliers and silk stockings, at which he had been railing, as he would have been in an American forest, making one in an Indian ring, by the light of a blazing fire, even though his hand had been locked in that of the most beautiful squaw that had ever listened to the roar of Niagara.

Nor was Peacock always sceptical about human motives. Sometimes his characters live up to their principles like Mr

Forester in *Melincourt*, who refuses to eat sugar because it is grown in the West Indies by slave labour. Sometimes Peacock shows practice failing to match theory through bettering it, as in the following episode in the same novel. Mr Fax is either a disciple of Malthus or a caricature of Malthus himself. Anyhow he believes that over-population is the world-menace and that the reckless production of children brings its well-merited reward in poverty and starvation. Walking with Mr Forester, Mr Fax tells the story of how a neighbouring couple were ruined through trying to rear children on an insufficient competence, a highly moral example of the working of the Malthusian doctrine. Mr Fax ends his tale thus:

> I made more particular inquiry into their circumstances, and they at length communicated to me, but with manifest reluctance, that they were in imminent danger of being deprived of their miserable furniture and turned out of their wretched habitation, by Lawrence Litigate, Esquire, their landlord, for arrears of rent amounting to five pounds.
> *Mr Forester*—Which, of course, you paid?
> *Mr Fax*—I did so: but I do not see that it is of course.

Perhaps what endears Peacock most to us is not so much his satirical contrasts between profession and practice as the contrasts and the fooleries that are just very good fun: the Rev. Mr Opimian at the wedding banquet at the end of *Gryll Grange* ordering a peal of "Bacchic ordnance" from the discharge of a volley of champagne corks or, in the *Misfortunes of Elphin*, the great drunkard Seithenyn collapsing after the effort of a tremendous speech in favour of keeping things as they are, or the very simple piece of comedy that follows this episode. Prince Elphin, to whom Seithenyn's eloquence had been directed, was left sober in the hubbub of the other's collapse. Angharad, Seithenyn's daughter, hearing the noise, enters the dining hall and directs the cup-bearers to carry out her father. Peacock goes on:

> Elphin gazed with delight on the beautiful apparition, whose gentle and serious loveliness contrasted so strikingly with the

broken trophies and fallen heroes of revelry that lay scattered at her feet.

"Stranger," she said, "this seems an unfitting place for you: let me conduct you where you will be more agreeably lodged."

"Still less should I deem it fitting for you, fair maiden," said Elphin.

She answered, "The pleasure of her father is the duty of Angharad."

Elphin was desirous to protract the conversation, and this very desire took from him the power of speaking to the purpose. He paused for a moment to collect his ideas, and Angharad stood still, in apparent expectation that he would show symptoms of following, in compliance with her invitation.

In this interval of silence he heard the loud dashing of the sea and the blustering of the wind through the apertures of the walls.

This supplied him with what has been, since Britain was Britain, the alpha and omega of British conversation. He said, "It seems a stormy night."

The enumeration, such as I have given, of the qualities that make Peacock's novels what they are is vain or at best accomplishes but a very little. For it is the way these qualities are blended that gives the novels their excellence. In this blending Peacock was probably helped by the short moral tales of the French eighteenth century, of which Voltaire's *Candide* is the most famous. And it may be that some readers feel Peacock a little alien, not altogether one of themselves. If they persisted even a very little they would lose their prejudice and find in Peacock an author not indeed of the first rank but able to give intense pleasure, and pleasure of a kind that can be found in the work of no other author.

This pleasure is of a most serious kind and has ultimately to do with civilisation; and I can applaud this sentiment from a recent book on the English novel:

Peacock is a novelist—one of a very small number—whose work attracts us more, and is increasingly more important, the longer the period of time since its first appearance; and as the existence of civilization becomes the more precarious, the more precious it will be.

Indeed, Peacock was confronted with the same difficulties that confront many of us today: that of behaving sanely in a world that is taking a course we heartily dislike. At a recent meeting of town planners in the United States it was reported that

> Prof. Richard L. Meier of the University of Chicago spoke in cheerful vein of the place of the automobile in tomorrow's world. He predicted cities will sprout "spokes" of 200 or more miles long, with the car an essential for the suburban dweller.

I cannot share Prof. Meier's cheerfulness about such cities or imagine any life in them other than semi-barbarous. Peacock felt much in the same way about the inventions of the industrial revolution. But he was never bitter in his feeling of opposition and he knew that you had to put up with and make the best of the innovations you disliked. In fact he followed the principles laid down in spendid Latin verse by another author who deplored his own age, Petrarch:

> Utendum sorte est, et sidera nostra sequenda
> Quo ducunt ne forte trahant.

> We must accept our destiny, we must follow the lead of our own stars lest they drag us in their wake.

Be critical, says Peacock, but never bitter. Accept the inevitable in matters of material progress but do not pander to it. Retain your faith in the pieties of the human mind, pieties that can be soiled by the wrong course of material things but which cannot be destroyed by them. That is Peacock's advice, and it seems to me as sound now as when he gave it. Though put so gaily and elegantly, it is sounder and more philosophical than the hysteria of *1984*; more like E. M. Forster's less known *The Machine Stops*. It is partly because they help us to be sane today that Peacock's novels are still so eminently worth reading.

The Origins of English Anti-Romanticism

IN England the first world war was culturally a greater interruption than the second. A bigger proportion of its rising young men—I mean the young men who would in the natural course of events have modified and shaped our literary heritage—found themselves in the front line than was the case in the second war, while in that front line the percentage of deaths was about twice as great. There was in fact a gap in culture comparable to that during the civil war in the seventeenth century, followed, as I shall point out, by a similar increase of foreign influences. These foreign influences had very different origins, but they were powerful in both seventeenth and twentieth centuries because in the gap the native tradition had weakened. One sign of weakness was that at the outset of the new settlements, in 1660 and 1918, people tried to continue literary habits as if there had been no gap. When the Restoration theatres opened, there were curious attempts (by Etheredge for instance) to continue the loose and debased blank verse that had been the medium of some drama in the years before the theatres were closed in 1642. In 1918 the common reader was unaware that the Romantic tradition was threatened. He accepted the unguarded emotionalism of Rupert Brooke and the inbred pictorial power that Flecker had inherited from Rossetti as true to the temper of the age, and he unconsciously set up Shelley and Keats as the standard of essential poetry. True, he had begun to hear of and then to read Donne but he had not yet been taught that you were not allowed to admire Donne and Shelley simultaneously. Grierson, whose edition of Donne in 1912 did so much to advance the reputation of this poet, had no quarrel with the Romantics as such; while the two other men who did most to popularise Donne in England before the war were Rupert Brooke himself and his friend and schoolfellow, Geoffrey Keynes.

Coming back from abroad in 1919, a lucky survivor from

the previous years and with a classical and not a modern literary upbringing, I shared the common ignorance of what had been going on behind the scenes and the common assumptions about the normality of English Romantic poetry; and I acquired Grierson's edition of Donne in the correct manner. Nor did I find that my pupils at Cambridge, nearly all of them ex-service men and candidates for the then infant English Tripos, assumed anything different. There were indeed rumours abroad of heretical views; but such rumours are endemic in a University: and it was not till an evening in the autumn of 1922 that I learnt that something new had begun and that the old assumptions about the Romantics were being seriously challenged. It was a supervision hour; and the topic for discussion was Shelley's *Ode to the West Wind*. Of the pair who came for supervision one was English, the other American. Now I was quite prepared for a pupil to say that he did not care for this particular poem or that he could not get on with Shelley. But these two young men very quickly let me know not only that they detested Shelley's Ode but that it was the wrong kind of poetry altogether. In fact I was in the same position as Justice Bolt in Crabbe's *Dumb Orators* when he found himself unexpectedly in a company of the opposite political persuasion to himself. I did, however, do what I could to defend Shelley's poem, which I did then genuinely admire and which I have never ceased to admire, against this sudden and, as then seemed, surprising attack. There was no doubt about the force of the attack. Here were two young men, intelligent and lively it is true but not of conspicuously original minds, laying down the law with an assured emphasis. Plainly, they had a powerful backing, of whatever kind. I conceived a curiosity about the nature of this backing and later I was able at least partially to satisfy it. The young men were the agents, or the apostles, or the victims—I leave you to choose whichever of these words you think appropriate—of a complicated combination of impulses, leading in the same direction but varying somewhat according to the nationality of the agent. What follows is my brief version of how these young men— or principally how the young Englishman—came to dislike the Romantic poets as such, when had he lived twenty years earlier he would have been at the same age their unquestioning admirer.

It must not be thought that the poets of the Romantic Revival have altogether lacked adverse criticism at any time. Certainly they got plenty of opposition in their own day. Here is a sample from as late a year as 1817; and it comes from a notice of Coleridge's *Christabel* from the *Monthly Review*:

> This precious production is not finished, but we are to have more and more of it in future! It would be truly astonishing that such rude unfashioned stuff should be tolerated, and still more that it should be praised by men of genius (witness Lord Byron and some others), were we not convinced that every principle of correct writing, as far as poetry is concerned, has been long *given up:* and that the observance, rather than the breach of such rules is considered as an incontrovertible proof of rank stupidity. It is grand, in a word, it is sublime, to be lawless; and whoever writes the wildest nonsense in the quickest and newest manner is the popular poet of the day!

This, of course, is a typical example of the criticism of fear, of the instinctive dread of the unknown, taking refuge in precedent. It is the kind that condemns all modern music because it is full of discord and modern art because it is ugly. There is a pleasant confirmation of the *Monthly Review's* opinion of *Christabel* in a note pencilled by an unknown hand after *Kubla Khan* in the copy of the first edition of *Christabel* now in the library of Jesus College, Cambridge. It runs: "Perfect Nonsense! The writer of the above had much better have kept his sleeping thoughts to himself, for they are, *if possible*, worse than his waking ones."

But there were profounder and more discerning critics than the two anonymous ones of Coleridge whom I have just quoted. There was Jane Austen, whose whole life and manner of writing were an implicit criticism of the whole Romantic movement. There was Peacock, the movement's most consistent satirist. There was Jeffrey, the most formidable and systematic opponent of the new poetical style.

Jeffrey was a fine specimen of eighteenth-century good sense, and his perception of the weak side of Romanticism has never been bettered. Here is his perception of the emotional exaggeration to which the Romantics have always been prone, from his review of Southey's *Thalaba*:

> Next after great familiarity of language there is nothing that appears to our modern poets so meritorious as perpetual exaggeration of thought. There must be nothing moderate, natural, or easy, about their sentiments. There must be a "qu'il mourût", and a "let there be light", in every line; and all their characters must be in agonies and ecstasies, from their entrance to their exit. . . . These authors appear to forget that a whole poem cannot be made up of striking passages; and that the sensations produced by sublimity are never so powerful and entire as when they are allowed to subside and revive, in a slow and spontaneous succession.

But Jeffrey was in opposition to the new and rising movement; and his good sense was interpreted as obscurantism; and an essay like Lamb's *Sanity of True Genius*, which is also a plea for good sense, coming from the rising party, was more likely to be effective in checking Romantic excess.

But the Romantics themselves were too busy fighting battles for their own cause against Augustan prejudice to spare much time on self-criticism. The first effective attack on Romanticism from within the movement comes after the middle of the nineteenth century; and to understand both it and later attacks in England we shall have to turn to France.

The triumph of Romanticism in France came later than it did in England, and the reaction against it began much earlier. Indeed one of the movement's most intimate members became one of its principal critics. We think of Sainte-Beuve chiefly as the great critic of the mid-nineteenth century and less as the man who in his youth was the friend of Victor Hugo and wrote a highly emotional erotic novel. Sainte-Beuve was both a man who risked becoming the prey of his emotions in a Rousseauish manner and the man gifted with a dreadfully impartial and penetrating intellect. And with this intellect he was unable to take the French Romanticists at their own estimate. As a judge of men he was tolerant, expecting little, and merciless, shrinking from no revelation. He found the French authors who wrote like gods, Chateaubriand and Hugo, ungodlike as men and less godlike as authors than they fancied. And then he was learned and he understood so much about other literary epochs that he could not maintain the illusion that the Romanticists had the one true Gospel; he could not help seeing them in proportion, in their relation to other schools of writing. And this was new, because others had either a Romantic or an anti-Romantic bias. Sainte-Beuve kept his head; he was critical of the movement but without condemning it wholesale like the Monthly Reviewer of *Christabel*. Well, Sainte-Beuve wrote impartially of Chateaubriand and praised Racine in the 1840's; and there is little doubt that he encouraged Matthew Arnold to try to be properly critical of the great English Romantic movement of which he was the heir. It was with the sense of Sainte-Beuve in the background that Arnold was able in his preface to his 1853 volume of poems to repeat Jeffrey's accusation of the Romantics as being too lavish of brilliant effects, of spoiling the whole for the parts. And it may well be his sense of Sainte-Beuve's great learning and catholic literary taste that prompted him in a later essay to accuse the English Romantic movement of being premature, supported by an insufficient critical effort, and not knowing enough. That was all very well, but Arnold's own creative writing was not revolutionary and by composing poetry on the whole in the Romantic idiom he really condoned the movement he professed to criticise. Moreover, Arnold was isolated in his criticism; he had no followers in it: and to understand later English attacks on the Romantics we have to return to France. And I shall have to make a few generalisations about French literature in the nineteenth century in order to explain those French attacks on Romanticism which I believe to be at the back (however little they were aware of it) of my two pupils when they vented their distaste of Shelley's *Ode to the West Wind*.

It is roughly true of French poetry that after the Hugo-esque effervescence had subsided it imposed a high formal excellence on the now accepted Romantic subject-matter. The Romantic poets had been prone to create pictures in poetry and to explore the recesses and the crannies and the involutions of their own minds. This proneness was continued by the successors of the first Romanticists, Gautier and Baudelaire; and the high standard of their technique averted the kind of criticism to which the looser techniques of Lamartine, Hugo, and Musset might have been open. Flaubert represents a corresponding tightening of technique in the novel. The result was that in France there was little occasion for a partial, Arnoldian attack on grounds of lushness or carelessness. Without a questioning of the validity of the whole Romantic subject-matter, nothing could happen. On the other hand there were strong reasons why such a questioning should begin in France rather than in England.

First, the Romantic movement in France was at once more extreme and less suited to the national temper than the corresponding movement in England. It worked up to its climax in the hectic and disillusioned years that followed Waterloo and was in its exaggerated spirit nearer to the excesses of Byron, Poe, and Swinburne than to Wordsworth and Keats. It is true that Mario Praz and F. L. Lucas have collected abundant examples of Romantic excess from both countries; nevertheless the following comparison represents something near the truth. Keats professed the cult of the sensations and practised tricks like peppering his tongue to make claret taste more interesting. But such a cult was mild and peripheral. Musset in his *Confessions d'un Enfant du Siècle*, that brilliant picture of post-Napoleonic France, betrays a neurosis far deeper-seated than any sensation-hunting found in Keats. He recounts for instance how he used to wear his mistress's miniature over his heart. In order to get a masochistic pleasure he mounted it on a metal disc studded with sharp points. These, stabbing him with every movement he made, caused such curious pleasure that sometimes he pressed the spikes in with his hand to heighten the voluptuousness. Well, Romanticism, being more extreme in France, was the more liable to attack.

Secondly, literature in France has always been more

closely allied with politics than in England. And, from the first, French Romanticism was allied with the principles of the French Revolution. A single instance will suffice to show how different was the case in England. Tennyson was the heir of the Romantic tradition of poetry through Coleridge and Keats; in his own age he was central to it: yet he was in no sense a revolutionary or even a radical in politics but a firm supporter of Church and King. In France, with literature and politics connected, it was inevitable that any reaction there against democracy should also be a reaction against the Romantic tradition in literature.

The reaction itself in France was many-sided and is quite beyond my scope in a single lecture. When something new happens in literature it will show itself simultaneously in creative writing and in criticism; and it is impossible to say which comes first. One type of writing will encourage the other; there will be a constant to-and-fro process. I shall here confine myself mainly to the more academic side of critical thought: a side which had a powerful effect on English opinion, though only after a long delay and through devious channels.

The academic attacks on the Romantic tradition in France first centre in Ferdinand Brunetière. Brunetière (1849-1906) was exceptionally influential as both holding a high academic position in the École Normale Supérieure and editing the *Revue des deux Mondes*. He was a man of powerful and decided character, unafraid of giving offence; a real leader. And his opinions were simple and uncompromising. He believed the whole Romantic movement to be fundamentally vicious. *Classical* and *Romantic* for him meant *social* and *individual*. He believed further that the French genius was social and that the Romantic movement was fundamentally vicious in having surrendered order and sound manners to the unrestrained indulgence of individual caprice. He could see only one cure: the imposition of external authority. In literature he wanted a new literary dictator, a second Boileau. Late in life he joined the Catholic Church as the one institution that provided an arbitrary moral standard. Brunetière was a strong man, with a massive intellect and an emphatic style. He was at the height of his power in the early 1890s, a great figure in Paris, a man who just could not be ignored whether by friend or foe. And his influence was not confined to France. Academically, Brunetière's faction was a minority. It is said that when Pierre Lasserre, one of that faction, submitted his *Romantisme Français* as his thesis for the *Doctorat ès Lettres* at the Sorbonne it narrowly missed being turned down through sheer partisan hostility. This book, published in 1907, is a splendid piece of sustained criticism, critical of the French Romanticists but anxious to give them what credit is really their due.

I return now to England, though I shall have to bring in France once again.

Matthew Arnold was very much an Oxford man, and I suspect that what faint anti-Romanticism persisted in the late nineteenth century in England was primarily connected with that University. An interesting figure is Courthope (1842-1917), author of a history of English poetry and Professor of Poetry at Oxford. Courthope had a genuine liking for literature and a clear, robust, undistinguished mind. He stated his critical position in his inaugural lecture at Oxford in 1895, subsequently published in *Life in Poetry, Law in Taste*. In all respects he is a Tory. There must, he held, be discipline and standards in literature; and these are supplied by the great writers of the past. Further, a writer must not be purely individual; he must speak for his own age. Such sentiments seem at first sight akin to what Brunetière was preaching at this time in Paris; yet Courthope drew very different conclusions. He did not attack the whole Romantic movement as unsound. On the contrary, he approved of the great English Romantic poets, considering that they did indeed speak for their age. But he is hostile to modern introspection and praises Kipling for having got back to real life. That shows his weakness. Provided that introspection is made respectable by age, as in the *Prelude*, he condones it. He has not got the force of conviction to say that the *Prelude* shows an evil, introverted, tendency, even if it has poetic merit. Courthope, then, was not like Brunetière, a man who would not compromise, a leader; and it was some years before Oxford put up an effective questioning of the Romantic tradition.

In 1896 and 1897 David Nichol Smith, who had just finished his studies at Edinburgh, was at Paris with a travelling fellowship from his University. There he spent his time learning what were the most live trends of French academic thought; and it is very relevant to my theme that Brunetière was the occasion of his first book. It appeared in 1898 and is entitled *Brunetière's Essays in French Literature. A Selection. Translated by D. Nichol Smith. With a Preface by the Author for this, the authorised English Translation.* And in the same year Nichol Smith published an edition of Boileau's *Art Poétique.* Later he became a Lecturer at Glasgow, where Walter Raleigh was Professor. It was this association with Raleigh that a few years later was to make the English School at Oxford an influential if restrained agent of less unguardedly enthusiastic and more critical opinions of the English Romantics. The method of Raleigh and Nichol Smith was less to attack the Romantics than to point out that the eighteenth century had virtues which the Romantics had forfeited. A classic example is Raleigh's comparison of the Shakespeare criticism of the two periods. This was published in 1908, the year Nichol Smith joined Raleigh at Oxford, in an essay that was subsequently to become one of *Six Essays on Johnson.* Speaking of two passages of Shakespeare criticism, one from Johnson, the other from Coleridge, Raleigh said:

The romantic attitude begins to be fatiguing. The great romantic critics, when they are writing at their best, do succeed in communicating to the reader those thrills of wonder and exaltation which they have felt in contact with Shakespeare's imaginative work. This is not a little thing to do; but it cannot be done continuously, and it has furnished the work-a-day critic with a vicious model. There is a taint of insincerity about romantic criticism, from which not even the great romantics are free. They are never in danger from the pitfalls that waylay the plodding critic; but they are always falling upward, as it were, into vacuity. They love to lose themselves in an *O altitudo.* From the most worthless material

they will fashion a new hasty altar to the unknown God. . . .
Those who approach the study of Shakespeare under the sober
and vigorous guidance of Johnson will meet with fewer exciting
adventures, but they will not see less of the subject.

Raleigh's attack on Romantic criticism resembles Jeffrey's
attack on the Romantic poets I quoted near the beginning of
this lecture; and it may not be an accident that two years
after it there appeared this volume: *Jeffrey's Literary Criticism. Edited with Introduction by D. Nichol Smith.* These
Oxford doctrines were not revolutionary. They did not attack
the Romantic poets as a group. If they disliked Shelley,
they praised Wordsworth. But they were highly critical and
in a quiet way had a powerful influence.

The other chief academic centre of English anti-
Romanticism was Harvard, where its exponent was Irving
Babbitt. Babbitt was Professor of French and the author of a
standard book on French criticism of the nineteenth century.
He knew what Brunetière stood for and in many ways was
his opposite number in the English-speaking countries. He
was like Brunetière in treating the Romantic tradition as not
merely a literary but a moral offence, and he was like him in
his rugged personality. Babbitt disapproved of the English
Romantic poets chiefly for their naturalism, their sentimental
mysticism of nature which, as he thought, caused them to
upset the true human hierarchies and to subordinate the
human spirit to inanimate nature. He differed from Brunetière in the matter of liberty. He was born in Dayton, Ohio,
in 1865 and he believed in liberty of a sort. Anyhow he did
not agree with Brunetière on the need of an external discipline: that spelt atrophy and death. What was needed was
the internal check, a human self-discipline. He believed in
humanism not in an imposed religious authority. The present
point is that he thought the Romanticists lacked the inner
check; they were undisciplined and no true humanists.
Babbitt, like Brunetière in Paris, was in opposition at
Harvard, partly because of his creed and partly because of
his dogmatic unyielding temper, but he was a powerful
influence. Another great man on the Harvard staff, Santa-

yana, was also an influence against the excessive admiration
of the Romantics. His splendid chapter on the Poetry of
Barbarism in *Interpretations of Poetry and Religion* reinforces
Babbitt on the Romantic lack of discipline. But Santayana
was so many-sided that he will never be closely associated
with anti-Romanticism; he is too big a man for any such
exclusive relation. Babbitt, on the other hand, had both the
drive and the limitations of the man with only one mastering
idea.

For the latest phase, the phase that was behind the
opinions of the two undergraduates from whom I began, I
must return briefly to France. Brunetière's attack on the
French Romantics had been literary and moral mainly, not
political. But after him political passions worked strongly
against them. In the early twentieth century French democracy suffered severe attacks from both Left and Right.
Georges Sorel, the philosophical syndicalist, born as far back
as 1847 but at the height of his activity in the first years of
this century, violently attacked not only democracy but
Romanticism is his *Réflexions sur la Violence*. On the other
wing were the French royalists, led by Charles Maurras,
who identified Classicism with Gallicism and civilisation,
Romanticism with Teutonism (the Anglo-Saxon variety
included) and barbarism. Their complete range was to be
Catholic in religion, royalist in politics, and classicist in
literature.

I have spoken of Oxford and Harvard. And now the
University of Cambridge comes into the picture, though in
a smaller way. One of the conspicuous personalities at
Cambridge before the first world war was T. E. Hulme. His
presence there was fitful, but he made himself felt. And when
he was in the army he continued his connection with Cambridge by contributing to the *Cambridge Magazine*, under
the name of North Staffs, articles on the war's progress.
Hulme's activities were various. He was the chief critical
influence on the group of poets who called themselves
Imagists; he lived in several countries on the Continent and
was anything but insular; he translated Sorel's *Réflections sur
la Violence*. But above all he represented a radical programme

which condemned not merely the Romantic Revival but the whole trend of thought from the Renaissance onwards as being grossly realistic and unspiritual and sharply opposed to the spirituality of the Middle Ages and the noble abstraction of Byzantium. I think that echoes of what T. E. Hulme had been preaching to little groups of advanced young men just before the first world war must have been heard in the Cambridge of 1918 onwards and have reached, in some form or other, the ears of my two undergraduate pupils.

Yet the prime agent for mediating these and the other ideas of which I have spoken, in the years 1919-1922, was T. S. Eliot; and it is worth reflecting how many of these ideas he had experience of. As a man greatly influenced by Babbitt at Harvard he was aware of the anti-Romanticism of him and of Brunetière. At Oxford he was open to the proclivity to rehabilitate the Augustan age and to depress the Romantic. As a young poet associated, though not at all identified, with the Imagists he knew Hulme and what he stood for. He was of course well aware of French literature and thought, quite apart from Hulme. His own early poetry was particularly influenced by Laforgue, a poet who forsook the rhetoric and the hieratic pretensions of the Romantic School and who exploited the ordinary world in an apparently cool and ironic tone without forgoing a fundamentally poetic treatment. And when in 1927 Eliot called his general point of view "classicist in literature, royalist in politics, and Anglo-Catholic in religion" he was repeating with a modification the formula of Maurras and his associates. But though Eliot was the chief agent for popularising the anti-Romantic doctrine among the advanced young intellectuals in those years and though he was in some ways a pioneer, he was also a mouth-piece for conceptions that had been maturing for years and in whose creation he had no hand. My two pupils had probably been collecting unawares all sorts of hints of the things they were to learn explicitly from the writings and the talk of T. S. Eliot. But whether or not they had gone through this process of preparation, they were inheriting through T. S. Eliot a complex of ideas of whose history and multiplicity they had not the least conception.

I return finally to the comparison with which I began: that between the situations in 1660 and 1918 in England. When the English court returned from exile in 1660 it had acquired many of the critical ideas that had dominated France in the years after Richelieu founded the French Academy in 1635, including a belief in the barbarism of the literature of any period less sophisticated than the modern. But ultimately the French influence dwindled, and English writers were drawn to some of the writings that belonged to their own barbaric past. Dryden gave up rhyme in tragedy and rewrote Shakespeare's *Antony and Cleopatra*. If anything has emerged from my brief survey it is how much English anti-Romanticism owes to France. Here the resemblance with 1660 is strong. But there is an important factor absent in the seventeenth century. During the years when the reaction against the English Romantics was growing, a big proportion of the influential writers in the English language were not English: Yeats, Joyce, Henry James, Eliot. The specifically English tradition was attenuated, with a smaller probability of a counter-movement back to the English Romantics. Of the authors dealt with by Edmund Wilson in his *Axel's Castle*, that very influential volume dealing with imaginative literature 1870-1930, not one was British born. And Wilson published his book in 1931, when the reaction against Romanticism was at its height.

Of course, it may be that the early twentieth century witnessed one of those few definitive changes in the direction of thought and that there will be no return to the freer emotionalism of the Romantic age. But I do not think we yet know. Rupert Brooke's poems have had a large steady sale through all the years when the intellectuals have held him up to obsecration. Walter de la Mare, so English and so little revolutionary in technique and yet so free from the characteristic vices of the Romantic tradition, has maintained a steady popularity. Rex Warner and Joyce Cary, though of little influence compared with certain non-British novelists, are in the English tradition and little affected by outside influence in their technique. I believe it still possible that the breach is smaller than supposed, that a native way of writing may regain its vigour, and that the year of the Festival of Britain may in the end be found to have more continuity with the year of the Great Exhibition than at the moment seems, on a close view, to be in the least likely.

Conrad's "Secret Agent" Reconsidered

RESPONSES to Conrad's *Secret Agent* have ranged from total capitulation to coolish approval; and it is not yet at all clear what position in the future hierarchy of his works this novel is destined to occupy. A reconsideration needs no apology.

First, we can accept the virtue of the writing throughout and of the different scenes considered in themselves as scenes. Any blemishes here are incidental. We may tire of hearing Comrade Ossipon called "robust" and we may find a speech or two of the Assistant Commissioner to the Home Secretary (in spite of the latter's appeal for brevity) clotted and obscure. And of course there are the mistakes in English. But all these are small matters; and the only serious mistake of detail is in the psychology of Ossipon. Granted his previous presentation, is it likely that he would have been haunted permanently by the thought of Mrs Verloc's death and been permanently put off his amorous adventures? I can find nothing in his previous states of mind to justify such fidelity to an impression. I suspect that Conrad here unconsciously sacrificed psychological probability to certain demands of plot to which I shall refer later. But in its context of the last chapter this blemish does not count for much; it affects our pleasure in reading very little, for it co-exists with so much else to think about.

Next, I can only concur in most of the praise that writers have bestowed on Conrad's ironic method, on his success in keeping his dreadful story within the bounds of comedy. His constant ironic method is to keep very large the distance between the way things appear to the persons in the story and the way they are made to appear to the reader. A typical instance is the theme of Verloc's hat. Verloc's hat and overcoat, constantly worn indoors, are powerful instruments for building up Verloc's character; they are symbols of his physical and mental frowstiness. Then, rather more than half way through the book, Conrad gives us the reasons for Verloc's habit of wearing hat and overcoat indoors. "It was not devotion to an outdoor life, but the frequentation of foreign cafés which was responsible for that habit, investing with a character of unceremonious impermanency Mr Verloc's steady fidelity to his own fireside." And of course Verloc has no notion of this discrepancy between appearance and reality. The culminating chapter containing the murder ends thus:

> Then all became still. Mrs Verloc on reaching the door had stopped. A round hat disclosed in the middle of the floor by the moving of the table rocked slightly on its crown in the wind of her flight.

These words are perfect in deflating the murder—that is as it concerns the victim. The grotesque rocking of the inverted bowler indeed resembles and mocks Verloc's precarious state of mind in the last weeks, just as its dethronement from the eminence of his head duplicates and minimises his own downfall. The hat figures for the last time when Ossipon, now convinced that he is the victim of a plot to murder him, returns with Winnie Verloc to the house in Brett Street. He is standing in the shop looking through the glass of the door into the parlour, where Verloc lies, apparently asleep, Ossipon still under the illusion that he had been blown to pieces in Greenwich Park:

> But the true sense of the scene he was beholding came to Ossipon through the contemplation of the hat. It seemed an extraordinary thing, an ominous object, a sign. Black and rim upward, it lay on the floor before the couch as if prepared to receive the contributions of pence from people who would come presently to behold Mr Verloc in the fullness of his domestic ease reposing on a sofa.

There is, of course, more than one kind of irony here. For instance, there is the contrast between the appearance of domestic ease and the reality of its opposite. But the main irony consists in the fantastic distance between what Conrad instructs the reader to think of, the likeness of the hat to a beggar's inviting coins, and Ossipon's vision of it as a symbol of chaos come again. And by achieving that distance Conrad makes the reader very happy indeed.

In general, too, Conrad is tactful in his use of this ironic tool. Winnie Verloc is pathetic and even noble. It would be a piece of very bad taste to submit her to the kind and the degree of ridicule that is apt for her husband. Nevertheless she cannot be allowed to engage our sympathies too tenaciously, or the whole tone of the book will be ruined. So in the murder scene, where her sufferings are great, Conrad avoids irony as far as she is concerned and concentrates on reducing the scale of the potentially tragic action. Before the scene he had kept on insisting that her view into things did not go deep, as when he tells us that "Mrs Verloc wasted no portion of this transient life in seeking for fundamental information." And this insistence is continued into the scene itself with such remarks as, "The visions of Mrs Verloc lacked nobility and magnificence." She is indeed a woman with small range of mind, incapable of holding more than one important thing in it at the same time. Hatred of Verloc as the murderer of Stevie at first quite usurps it, to be expelled by her use of the carving-knife. Then the vision of the gallows takes complete possession. In her extremity she is too ignorant to know how to escape abroad. By such means Conrad succeeds in rendering innocuous the powerful sympathies the reader might have had with her obsessive devotion to her helpless brother. And that devotion too had come in for its share of criticism before the catastrophe, for it is short-sighted devotion, preventing Winnie from seeing why her mother had left Brett Street for the almshouse. Thus Conrad contrives to deflate Mrs Verloc, but without the impropriety of an ironic method of deflation. He does something similar before her suicide, which in its turn must not be allowed to cross the borderline into tragedy. The scene that follows Mrs Verloc's flight from her house and her accidental encounter with Ossipon is both macabre and richly comic. And the comedy is that of cross purposes and mutual misunderstanding. Thinking that it is Verloc who was blown up and ignorant of the murder, Ossipon first believes that Winnie is a genuine pick-up or windfall and prepares to make use of his good luck. But he soon sees he is wrong and flies to the opposite error of diagnosing her as a homicidal maniac, from whom at all costs he must escape. But Conrad is able, and without impropriety, to include Winnie in the comic context and in so doing to spotlight her stupidity. The climax comes when, waiting for the Southampton train to leave, she misinterprets Ossipon's words about Stevie.

"He was an extraordinary lad, that brother of yours. Most interesting to study. A perfect type in a way. Perfect."

He spoke scientifically in his secret fear. And Mrs Verloc, hearing these words of commendation vouchsafed to her beloved dead, swayed forward with a flicker of light in her sombre eyes, like a ray of sunshine heralding a tempest of rain.

"He was that indeed," she whispered softly, with quivering lips. "You took a lot of notice of him, Tom. I loved you for it."

After Mrs Verloc has reached that degree of stupidity, of grossness of misapprehension, we cannot think of her suicide as a tragic event.

But the *Secret Agent* is pervaded by another kind of irony, one that helps towards making the book a unity. It is the irony of great plans having trivial results and of the weightiest results being effected by trivial means. It is the kind of irony that encourages men to keep their eyes open and not to expect too much logic and tidiness from life; and Shakespeare gave it its classic embodiment in *Much Ado About Nothing*. There Claudio and Hero are the chief figures in the main plot although they are less fitted to be so than Benedick and Beatrice. Through a freak of fate their story nearly ends in disaster, but not quite. They arouse unnecessary passions in other people, and all the pains that these folk take to clear up the trouble are futile because the fantastic incompetence of Dogberry and his fellows anticipates the carefully directed efforts of their betters: "What your wisdoms could not discover, these shallow fools have brought to light." Beatrice, the potentially tragic figure, with a brilliant intellect, not only wastes her efforts in setting Benedick against Claudio, but has her love awakened by a trick that a less brilliant person might well have evaded; while the very trick may have been superfluous since Benedick and Beatrice are in fact deeply attracted to each other. Conrad writes in the mode of *Much Ado*; and, since this seems to be a new contention, I had better go into the details.

The first hint of expectations being falsified occurs in the opening scene at the (German or Austrian?) Embassy. There Privy Councillor Wurmt questions the vigilance of the English police, a vigilance which turns out to be embarrassingly greater than he had ever expected. Later, in the same scene, Vladimir announces that England must be brought into line with the Continent in the way she deals with revolutionaries: in the end his action only helps to perpetuate the difference of methods. Chief Inspector Heat hopes to use the explosion of the bomb to justify the imprisonment of Michaelis, whom he dislikes seeing at large; but this dislike awakens the suspicions of his superior and leads to a rebuff. The domestic set-up of the Verlocs is a humble and small-scale affair yet it makes itself felt in embassies and offices of state; while in turn the feelings there aroused are destined to lead nowhere. The mother of Mrs Verloc, thinking that her presence in the Brett Street house may ultimately annoy Mr Verloc and finally lead to his turning against her mentally deficient son, heroically contrives to retire to an almshouse. Her act is rich in unforeseen consequences. It leads first to Mr Verloc's taking more notice of Stevie and of finally using him to deposit the bomb that blows him up and second to Winnie's sewing the address of the house under Stevie's coat-collar, an act which identifies him as the blown-up man. Mrs Verloc did another thing to help Stevie. She joined with her daughter in impressing on him the measureless "goodness" of Mr Verloc. Thus impressed they thought he would be more docile in Mr Verloc's presence and hence more acceptable. It was through his blindly loyal belief in this "goodness" that Stevie let himself be persuaded to carry the bomb and so meet his death. The Assistant Commissioner of

Police hoped that the Greenwich explosion might become a *cause célèbre* and show up the iniquities of foreign embassies; and immediately, with Verloc's death, it lapsed into impenetrable obscurity. Most obvious of all, Verloc's efforts to pacify Winnie over Stevie's death serve instead to enrage her into committing murder. And lastly there is Ossipon, whose exposure to the same process is the *coda* of the novel. Ossipon, as well as affecting to be a revolutionary, was the *gigolo* of a steady succession of mature women not without means. He expected Winnie Verloc, widow of a man obviously possessed of means, to take her place in the succession. Finding her a murderess and haunted by the horror of her end, he is put off women altogether and takes to drink instead. I have questioned the motivation of this part of the novel but in ironic idea it is strictly in accord with the rest. Thus, the theme of ends miscarrying goes right through and can hardly not have been deliberately introduced by its author, and as a means towards unity of impression.

Conrad used yet another means towards that end: he constantly makes an earlier passage or episode presage a later. I can be brief here, for the critics are well aware of this. The following examples will be sufficient in illustration. When Stevie was tried for an office job, the other boys worked on his feelings and induced him to let off fireworks on the stairs. Their persuasiveness presages Verloc's influence on Stevie, as the fireworks presage the enlarged explosive that caused his death. The effect of the fireworks in the building was sensational: "silk hats and elderly business men could be seen rolling independently down the stairs": and it presages the sensation in other places where silk hats are worn—embassies and government departments—after the bomb went off in Greenwich Park. The conversation between the Verlocs at the end of the third chapter prepares us for the conversation that leads up to the murder. While Adolf is obsessed by the orders of Mr Vladimir, Winnie is obsessed by her anxiety over Stevie. Neither will listen to the other; both are quite self-absorbed. Near the end Winnie says she has had to take the carving knife from Stevie in his excitement, the same knife she later used to stick into Adolf.

All Winnie can achieve in the way of curiosity over her husband's troubles is the sleepy remark at the end, "Comfortable, dear? shall I put the light out now?"

II

I might have remarked at the end of the last paragraph that the cross-references are rarer in the parts concerning the police, as I could have remarked earlier that in those same parts there occurs a conspicuous exception to Conrad's usual ironic methods. Both remarks could have served to introduce the rest of this essay, which questions whether Conrad achieved the unity he intended. I will not support my first assertion, for this would involve the intolerable boredom of giving a list of certain or possible examples; but I shall have to explain in a little detail that Conrad suspends his ironic method in dealing with the Assistant Commissioner and perhaps also with the Home Secretary.

As first presented, the Assistant Commissioner might well be within the scope of Conrad's ironic method:

> At headquarters the Chief Inspector was admitted at once to the Assistant Commissioner's private room. He found him, pen in hand, bent over a great table bestrewn with papers, as if worshipping an enormous double inkstand of bronze and crystal. Speaking tubes resembling snakes were tied by the heads to the back of the Assistant Commissioner's wooden arm-chair, and their gaping mouths seemed ready to bite his elbows.

Here we might easily think of the Commissioner as an unconscious Laocoön caught in the coils of officialdom. But very soon we learn that he is as well aware of the coils as we are and as averse to them as Conrad would like his readers to be. The ironic distance between character and reader has been closed. Far from welcoming the sedentary imprisonment of administration, the Assistant Commissioner had an adventurous nature and would have preferred an active post in the tropics, such as he once had. He is denied his wish because, in a moment of blindness alien to his usual discriminating nature, he has married the wrong woman. Here is a perfect opportunity for the ironic method; but Conrad passes it by, allowing the Commissioner to have his own ironic situation quite under control:

> Chained to a desk in the thick of four millions of men, he considered himself the victim of an ironic fate—the same, no doubt, which had brought about his marriage with a woman exceptionally sensitive in the matter of colonial climate, besides other limitations testifying to the delicacy of her nature.

In fact, far from distancing him Conrad creates in the Assistant Commissioner a man much to his own liking. With the Home Secretary the case is slightly different. His physique and his clothes receive ironic treatment, presenting themselves to us and to himself differently, as when we learn that "the eyes, with puffy lower lids, stared with a haughty droop on each side of a hooked, aggressive nose, nobly salient in the vast pale circumference of the face." But there is nothing ironic in the way Conrad tells us how he coped with the problem presented to him by the Assistant Commissioner.

Not only does the Assistant Commissioner dodge outside the target of Conrad's irony; he is the one person whose plans do not miscarry. True, he had hoped, as I have noted, that the Greenich Park bomb would be the occasion of a *cause célèbre*, and his hopes were disappointed. But he scores substantial successes. He brings his subordinate to heel, as his two predecessors had failed to do; he had at last (in spite of his wife) been caught up in a job with a spice of adventure in it; and he flattened Mr Vladimir of the foreign embassy whose methods of dealing with revolutionaries he abhorred. Conrad dismisses him with, "He had had a full evening." He might with equal truth have added "and a very successful day."

These matters, little touched on by the critics, have their bearing on the better known dispute as to whether or not the police scenes are integrated with the rest, which is almost identical with the dispute about unity. Of course Conrad had every right to bring in the police. Anarchists are among the characters; a bomb was exploded: the police had a double justification to be present. The questions remain: do the police and their activities harmonise with the rest of the novel? are they to scale? Chief Inspector Heat is in keeping with the novel's dominant trend. He is presented ironically, and his plans turned out not as he expected. But we have seen that it is far otherwise with his superior: the Assistant Commissioner is not in keeping with the whole. Set against his subordinate he is admirable for the time begin, for the detached scene; but that excellence does not extend to the whole book. It looks as if Conrad's short term interest in him prevailed over his regard for the whole. Then there is the question of scale. The affairs of the police are largely concentrated into a long section of three consecutive chapters (V, VI, VII). They are brilliantly presented and they engage our attention and sympathy very deeply. In fact they whet our appetite for more. And we do get more in chapters IX and X. And yet somehow this addition does not satisfy; it does not suffice the appetite set up. The two chief characters have been elaborated too successfully; they have reached statures that demand scope in some major action and then perforce they have to dwindle into subordination to the affairs of the Verlocs. The disappointment is felt acutely when their direct interference in the action ends;

> The Assistant Commissioner himself did not turn into the noble building. It was the Explorers' Club. The thought passed through his mind that Mr Vladimir, honorary member, would not be seen very often there in the future. He looked at his watch. It was only half-past ten. He had had a very full evening.

This is a feeble dismissal, as if Conrad had no faith in it. "Yes," we feel like saying, "it is only half-past ten and you led us to believe that you would prolong these fascinating men's doings to midnight at least, if not into the small hours. You have let us down." Troubled by such thoughts and by the incongruity of the treatment given to the Assistant Commissioner, we cannot but conclude that the theme of the police is not perfectly integrated with that of the Verlocs.

The majestic scale of the scenes between the two police officers prompts a last doubt as to the perfection of the *Secret Agent*. Is not the scale of the scene-units too big for the scale of the whole? Conrad called his novel "a simple tale," and it is nothing of the kind. He may have meant it to be, but when it came to the execution he wove a complex plot and gave us some highly developed characters. More important, he worked through a series of massive, long-drawn-out scenes. It would be wrong to complain of the length of the culminating scene ending in the murder; but should it have been matched by scenes equally massive? Think of the long opening scene in the Embassy, of the intricate sparring between Heat and his superior, of the cab drive from Brett Street to the almshouses. I believe that Conrad, intending a simple ironic tale, could not resist the urge to employ the technique of the long novel, and allowed the supporting incidents to acquire an excessive consequence, out of scale with the central theme.

The parts of the novel are so good that in the act of reading them we can scarcely bother with their scale and their relation to the whole. In the reading it would be sacrilege to find fault with the glorious abundance of Conrad's account of the cab ride. Further, Conrad makes his story so interesting that we are carried along with our critical exactions mollified. Then there are the various features making for unity that I mentioned in the first section of this essay. These help powerfully to distract us from the novel's failings. It is only when we have ceased reading and look back and reflect on the whole that our doubts arise and that we reach this conclusion: that with all its merits the *Secret Agent* hovers a little uneasily between the novel in the grand manner and the long short-story.

Is a New History of Criticism Possible?

Is a new history of criticism possible?—but should I not first put another question: are histories of criticism desirable? And not every lover of literature thinks they are. True, some interest in critical theory arises naturally in the minds of most people who have any real inclination to literature; usually when they are young and when new general ideas have a powerful attraction. The old basic questions of art and morality, of the differences between verse and prose forms, of the relation of content and expression, start up fresh and exciting to every new generation. But, the young enthusiast is apt to ask, what has our interest to do with *history*? What we want is the *truth*. This we can get better today than in the past, because we know more than our predecessors. We are just beginning to understand how the human mind works; and aesthetics is a department of psychology. Why, when we are so much better equipped, grub up man's painful and broken approximations to truth through the ages? What of any value can Aristotle and Sidney teach us that has not been incorporated in contemporary theory? Let us go straight to the whole truth or to the maximum portion of it available up to date.

The answer is that applicable to all attempts to get the quickest returns in life, to take life in unnatural concentration. And it is that in the end they fail, because they ignore the natural processes of digestion and assimilation. Except for the tiny fraction of people with a natural gift for theorising, critical theory, in itself, however thrilling at the outset, soon gets stale. And one is forced to the conclusion that most critical theory, for prolonged interest, needs a setting in time to support it.

Further, once critical theory is set in time a double process is generated. Seen in its historical setting, critical theory comes alive; seen through critical theory, the setting takes on new significance. You can understand and relish the critical theories of an age if you relate them to the literature of that age; and you can see what that literature is getting at if you understand under what critical suppositions it was created. And not only that. The very theory itself, apart from its contemporary application, acquires an interest *through* that very application. For illustration take the Renaissance and Augustan theory of decorum; more especially the theory that certain kinds of diction are suited to certain unalterable literary kinds. Here is a matter that at first sight is dead; something outmoded, irrelevant to writing today, and in its theory rudimentary. Yet if you bring it in contact with contemporary production it acquires a new life. Consider it in connection with Milton's lines on Hobson, with *Paradise Lost*, and with *Samson Agonistes*. Those lines on Hobson, with their rough rhythm and quasi-metaphysical wit, have sometimes been thought exceptional and alien to Milton. Actually this roughness is governed by contemporary ideas of decorum as strictly as are the epic sonorities and sustentions of *Paradise Lost* and the dignified yet less sustained rhythms of *Samson Agonistes*. Hobson was a homely character, and to celebrate him as for instance Dryden celebrated the memory of Oldham would have been indecorous. Or take Dryden himself. Read his own defence of the style of *Religio Laici* and consider the different styles of that poem, of *Annus Mirabilis*, and of the *Secular Masque*. What happens through these considerations? First, the theory comes alive because we see that in its own age it meant something. Secondly, some of the literature becomes clearer because we see the literary theory actually influencing production. But still a third thing happens. Through seeing how the theory of decorum worked in the seventeenth century we apprehend a living example of the general problem of how formal means should be used to meet certain mental ends or requirements.

The moral is that no piece of critical theory, however dead apparently, or irrelevant to present production, is uninteresting, provided it was really dominant and influential in its day. You can no more bring an indictment against a dominant critical belief than against a whole people.

Now if critical theory as seen in time is interesting, and if the history of criticism deals with critical theory as seen in time, the history of criticism has an initial chance of being interesting too.

But here someone might interpose: aren't you making a very sweeping and dubious assumption, namely that a history of criticism concerns the history of ideas about literature and not the history of the criticism of the texts? What about Addison on *Paradise Lost* and Coleridge on the beauties and defects of Wordsworth? The answer is that of course you could treat the extant examples of literary appreciation historically, but that such a history would be a much more patchy, a much less connected, and a much less interesting affair. Apart from a chunk of Aristophanes and a few spots of Plato, Longinus and Quintilian, there is practically no eminent literary appreciation in classical criticism: it just cannot compare with the amount of good critical theory. What I am debating is not what is the ideal history of criticism but whether a new and living history of criticism is possible at the present moment; so I confine my survey to the portion of the subject where the possibility is highest.

As far as I know, there has been only one comprehensive history of criticism, that of George Saintsbury. The more recent work of J. W. H. Atkins, though it may have corrected a number of errors and brought together new arrays of fact, does not make the historical impression. It is a survey rather than a history. What is it that makes Saintsbury's work a history? First Saintsbury is highly personal and hardly at all objective; and for the continuity required for the historical illusion the steady pressure of a definite personality is a great advantage. Secondly, he applies some definite if limited standards. Most of his history is of course learned gossip (once amusing) about the various critics. But Saintsbury was a disciple of Pater, a man of the nineties. He believed passionately that literature should please, not instruct, that the subject was irrelevant, only the manner counting. And he applies these beliefs to the critics' writings from the beginning to the end of his book. When he wrote, those beliefs were alive; and it was that life that made his book worth writing and interesting in its own day.

Now to write a history of *all* the questions of critical theory that have ever interested mankind would be to run to impossible length, while no man could make it interesting because it is only a fraction of these questions that would have a vital interest for himself. Therefore the only history of criticism that can really qualify as such must concern those questions of critical theory that are most alive when such a history is written.

If that is a correct conclusion, the intending historian of criticism must first decide what are the ruling questions of literary criticism today.

Saintsbury wrote in an age of unexampled literary individualism, when public morality had least to do with problems of art. What mattered in a given work was its unique quality or flavour, the thing that made it different from all other work: and Pater called this quality a work's *virtue*. Not only were separate works of art unique rather than partly coincident with others; but the artistic process was disconnected from all other processes, and artistic morality had nothing to do with any other morality. This individualising and separatist trend was not the only one, nor was it universally accepted. There co-existed, for instance, the tradition, usually fathered on Taine, of merging the work of art in its general setting of thought, while Matthew Arnold and Courthope were acutely aware of the public as well as of the private and personal nature of a work of art. None the less the individualising trend was dominant.

Now today, though critics would never deny the unique element in every work of art, they are much less exclusively interested in it than they were; and the trend has been to associate aesthetic matters with other matters in life. One of the militant reactors against the separatism of art was I. A. Richards, whose root-doctrine was that the psychological constitution of art was no different in quality, and only different in degree, from the mental experiences derived from eating one's dinner or stroking a cat. Having outlived its initial iconoclastic thrill, the theory has no longer much emotional appeal, but it truly illustrates a wider trend of thought. Another change has been in the relation of art and morality. Although no one now would agree to consider poetry as versified preaching, there is no hostility to Renaissance doctrines of art as conducing to virtue by showing men acting nobly and as averting vice by showing wicked men punished. Further there is now pervasive if often tacit and unformulated support for there being some connection between art and ethics. In this support, however, I doubt if there is much *positive* enthusiasm.

No, it is two rather different forms of this general associational trend that have the most emotional force today. First, there is the belief that no man's aesthetic theory is worth much unless it is a connected part of a wider philosophy of life, and from this belief comes the critical question of how this connection can be and has been made. And second (but really included in the first question) is the position of art, and hence of the artist, in society and the state.

I therefore conjecture that a history of criticism today should consist of an exposition, based on the latest research, of the opinions of the chief literary critics through the ages held together and made continuous by special attention to the above two questions. You cannot omit this wider exposition, for readers will go to a history of criticism for information, but you can make it more alive and acceptable as well as more continuous by dealing with special themes, by, as it were, giving this information the peculiar colour-blend belonging to those themes of critical theory that most live in men's minds today.

Such a method is bound to affect the emphasis put on the different critics; and the first thing to do is to guard against any assumption that the resulting emphases are wholly right in the sense that the greatest emphases will go to the greatest critics. For instance, I fancy that on the suggested hypotheses Samuel Johnson will get less than his usual emphasis and Benjamin Jonson more. Samuel Johnson's brilliant biographical perceptions, his flair for the great man, and his exposure of critical shams have not any very exciting connection with the place of art in society. But Ben Jonson's fragmentary critical dicta, most of them derivative and yet so thoroughly adopted and adapted as to be quite his own, and his characteristic theory of comedy are in vital contact with more general opinions on life. Nevertheless Ben Jonson's greater aptitude to present requirements is only temporary and does not turn him into a greater critic than his later namesake.

One result of the proposed new criteria is that different kinds of evidence will be used. Aristotle is one of the critics who will suffer no diminution of emphasis; and yet on what different grounds will his importance rest! At first sight he does not touch the question of the place of art in society and he establishes no linking up of poetry with ethics comparable to that of politics with ethics. We have been used to putting Aristotle's critical eminence in quite other terms: in those of his astonishing success in propounding the right critical questions and of his penetrating though as yet simple psychological insight into artistic processes. Indeed at first sight his critical method is more that of the scientist than of the philosopher. And yet by what he assumes and does not say he offers powerful testimony to the importance he believed the arts to hold in life. His testimony can best be perceived through contrasts. Consider the connotations of two pieces of Romantic criticism: Shelley's *Defence of Poetry* and Carlyle's section in *Heroes and Hero-Worship* on the hero as poet. Shelley makes magnificent claims for the poet's importance beyond the apparent province of his own work. The poet is one of the legislators, though unacknowledged as such, of the world. But there is something febrile in the way the claim is made: arguing not only the author's tendency to febrility but a genuine apprehension about the artist's place in contemporary society. An indifferent or hostile audience evokes a heightened and importunate tone. Carlyle, seeking to exalt the great poets to the eminence of the great men of action, somehow strains his voice and in so doing betrays the uncertainty of his cause. Now Aristotle does not arrogate to poetry any place of unusual exaltation; he simply takes it for granted as one of the concerns of the rational civilized human being. There is no need for him to justify it in relation to politics, for it is an instinct, based on two appetites as fundamental to human nature as the gregarious instinct, the appetite for imitation and that for harmony and rhythm. There is nothing in criticism to compare with this Aristotelian tone of certainty. And the reason is that he is just and only just old enough to belong to a society inheriting an unbroken tradition of art as a necessary activity of that society as a whole and, in whatever way, of each individual of it. Plato, it must be noticed, attacks art not for any lack of universality but because the admitted instinct on which it is founded is low in the hierarchy of the brain.

Take for a second example another classical critic, Longinus. Interest in him has centred mainly in two things: his exaltation of the passions and the brilliant perceptions contained in some of his remarks on classical texts. We have also enjoyed the paradox of the treatise on the Sublime being less used in the Romantic period when the passions were at a premium than in the early Augustan age when they were at a discount but when the reverence for all things Greek gave currency to what in itself would have been suspect. Thus Pope can with safety assume the accents of Longinus when praising the passionate tone of Homer. We have also enjoyed Longinus's remarks on Sappho's ode to the effect of its reconciling contraries, with their anticipation of Coleridge's theory of the imagination. But in our supposed new history we shall find these matters less interesting than Longinus's conception of the place of literature in life. We shall read his wonderful last chapter on the venality and corruption of the world in which he lived along with the passages in which he indulges in a positive hero-worship of the great literary figures of the past; whence we shall easily see that for Longinus great literature was a substitute religion, much after the manner attributed by his enemies to Matthew Arnold. And literature as substitute religion is a topic today with a genuine emotional force.

The period in the history of criticism whose interest will most appreciate is the Middle Ages. So far its criticism has had no great interest to any but specialists. Lovers of Dante may read the *De Vulgari Eloquio* and his epistle to Can Grande; and a few non-specialists with an interest in the language of poetry may enjoy the first for its researches in the language proper to poetry and relate it to similar linguistic problems in western Europe. But the treatises on rhetoric, which form the bulk of so-called medieval criticism, are for the non-specialist dead. I do not say they need always be so, but I have not detected in the present educated reading public the powerful predisposition for matters of rhetorical technique required to bring the dead to life. On the other hand the above reading public is more interested in the Middle Ages than it was a generation ago and would like to know what place literature really held in the life of the community. As far as I know this matter has never been thoroughly gone into; and its study would require much patience and tact. The evidence would be found, not in the treatises on rhetoric but in casual remarks, scattered prefaces, implications, even silences. Patience would be required to accumulate the evidence: very great tact in drawing conclusions. The result would be highly complicated and contradictory but extremely interesting. I doubt if the Church had any consistent opinion on literature, but surmise that she treated it sometimes as a useful ally and sometimes as a dangerous competitor after the manner so wonderfully expounded in Petrarch's *Secretum*. Where the Church was really at ease with literature was when she could be certain it was a subsidiary activity to be included under that ticket of honest mirth which Aquinas had pronounced necessary to the health of mankind. The Nun's Priest was on perfectly sure ground when he told his story of the cock and the fox. But the general conclusion would probably be found to support Comparetti when he said that "while the ancients are steadily hated and maligned as pagans, their works are assiduously read and studied, and they are looked up to by the most enlightened Christians as men of learning and genius." However, I am not now concerned with the conclusions themselves but with my belief that, whatever these are, the present generation is likely to be interested both in them themselves and in the work leading up to them.

One of the critics who will figure most prominently in the new history of criticism is Sidney. I suppose what we have most valued him for is the sheer delight in poetry and confidence in its worth that shine through the whole of the *Defence of Poesy*; and nothing is likely to alter such a valuation. But beyond this the *Defence* has been thought of as "a defence of romance rather than poetry" (Saintsbury), a useful summary of current Renaissance commonplaces, a means of introducing the latest Italianate critical ideas into England, and an interesting attempt to reconcile Plato and Aristotle. The new emphasis will be on Sidney's conspicuous success (unique in English critics of the Renaissance) in adjusting poetry to the other activities of life. Far from being a mere defence of romance, Sidney's notion that poetry goes beyond nature is securely linked to the living theology of the age. By excelling nature, by substituting a golden for a brazen world, poetry glimpses the paradise from which man fell and creates a world of which, though in actual life he cannot live up to it, he still has memories:

> Neither let it be deemed too saucy a comparison to balance the highest point of man's wit with the efficacy of Nature, but, rather give right honour to the heavenly Maker of that maker, who, having made man to his own likeness, set him beyond and over all the works of that second nature: which in nothing he showeth so much as in poetry, when, with the force of a divine breath, he bringeth things forth far surpassing her doings; with no small argument to the incredulous of that first accursed fall of Adam, sith our erected wit maketh us know what perfection is and yet our infected will keepeth us from reaching unto it.

That is one cardinal belief in Sidney, but there is the complementary belief that poetry is also a species of action urging men towards that very perfection which it is miraculously able to reveal.

> This purifying of wit, this enrichment of memory, enabling of judgment, and enlarging of conceit, which commonly we call learning, under what name soever it come forth or to what immediate end soever it be directed, the final end is, to lead and draw us to as high a perfection as our degenerate souls, made worse by their clayey lodgings, can be capable of.

And because poetry is the highest form of teaching it is a prime agent of forwarding this process. In no critic is the connection between a theory of poetry and a theory of life more triumphantly made than in Sidney.

My last example of how emphasis will be altered relates to Wordsworth. Here again the alteration should be to his benefit. Not that there can ever be any sense in making him out a greater critic than Coleridge. But hitherto criticism has centred mainly on those matters in which Coleridge was able to prove Wordsworth to be grievously wrong. This was largely Wordsworth's fault, for he did indeed, in his 1800 preface, give pride of place to those questions of rustic life, poetic diction, and relation of verse and prose over which he incurred the just censure of Coleridge. Raleigh in a brilliant and persuasive chapter in his *Wordsworth* defended Wordsworth on the ground that he did not quite mean what he said, that you could find a more plausible case by interpreting liberally and not pressing the letter of the text, and that Coleridge, though *technically* right, was *humanly* over-severe. Such a defence will count little compared with the change of emphasis which a new history of criticism is bound to make. Wordsworth on poetic diction is a critic improvising a defective defence of his own poetic innovations, a man finding the wrong reasons for the things which in his heart he knows to be right. He becomes a critic of universal validity when, dropping his special, personal theme, he seeks to answer the great general questions: What is a poet? To whom does he address himself? And in his answers he gives us his theory of the place held by the poet in society. He lays down the complementary, if contrasted, functions of the scientist and the poet, linking the poet to some of the most living thought of the age:

> The Poet, singing a song in which all human beings join with him, rejoices in the presence of truth as our visible friend and hourly companion. . . . The Poet is the rock of defence for human nature; an upholder and preserver, carrying everywhere with him relationship and love. In spite of difference of soil and climate, of language and manners, of laws and customs; in spite of things

silently gone out of mind, and things violently destroyed; the Poet binds together by passion and knowledge the vast empire of human society, as it is spread over the whole earth, and over all time.

That is passionately felt and spoken, and it is the very core of Wordsworth's great preface. The doctrine is that of revolutionary idealism; the brotherhood of man. Poetry is linked to society by being a supreme agent in promoting that brotherhood. To the present generation such a theory is far more exciting than the question of rustic life in poetry.

Such then is my case for a new history of criticism. Its writing would be a very hard task. The old critical texts would have to be scanned with new eyes; and those eyes might become blurred and weary in the task. Moreover, if the composition lasted very long, there is the risk that the premises on which the book was being written would have changed before the end was reached. The mountain in labour would risk giving birth not to a silly little mouse but to a gigantic fossil.

"*A Mirror for Magistrates*" Revisited

I DO not intend to plead that, as poetry, the *Mirror* has been seriously misjudged, my main business being with its interest and not with its beauty. Nevertheless, thinking that it is rather better as poetry than the average of modern criticism allows, I will by way of preface point to a few places, usually, if not inveterately, ignored, which can give pleasure to the reader.

Lily Campbell, whose editions I, of course, use and to whom every student of the *Mirror* is immeasurably indebted, calls John Dolman's solitary contribution (one of the 1563 additions) "probably the worst poetry in the *Mirror*."[1] C. S. Lewis, on the other hand, while calling Dolman's *Lord Hastings* unsatisfactory and immature, finds it the most promising part of the collection. Dolman

> understands better than any of his collaborators, better even than Sackville, what a poem ought to be. The other ghosts are mere mouthpieces of moral and political doctrine; but Dolman really tries by changes of mood and human inconsistencies to dramatize his Hastings. . . . The poem is confused, crowded, and uncomfortable. But it anticipates, in however dim a form, nearly every one of the excellences which were soon to be knocking at the door.[2]

In their ways both are right. Dolman can write very bad verse, crude and halting. But he has infused life into parts of his story. And I would go beyond Lewis in holding that he can achieve not only memorable lines but memorable passages. The most memorable is the passage describing Hastings's flight with his master, Edward IV, from Lynn and the sea voyage: the embarkation, the isolation on the ship at sea, the flight from enemy ships. Dolman is close to the real

[1] *A Mirror for Magistrates*, edited by Lily B. Campbell, 1938, p. 45.

[2] *English Literature in the Sixteenth Century*, 1954, pp. 243-4. Maurice Evans, *English Poetry in the Sixteenth Century*, 1955, p. 123, also praises Dolman's contribution.

happening. This is his account of the passengers' plight at sea:

> As banished wightes, such ioyes we mought have made,
> Easd of aye thretnyng death, that late we dradde.
> But once our countreyes syght (not care) exempt,
> No harboure shewying, that mought our feare relent,
> No covert cave, no shrubbe to shroud our lyves,
> No hollow wodde, no flyght, that oft depryves
> The myghty his pray, no Sanctuary left
> For exyled prynce, that shroudes eche slave from theft:

> In pryson pent, whose woddye walles to passe
> Of no lesse peryll than the dying was:
> With the Oceane moated, battered with the waves,
> (As chaynd at Oares the wretched Galley slaves
> At mercy sit of Sea and enmyes shott,
> And shonne with death what they with flyght may not)
> But greenysh waves, and desert lowrying Skyes
> All comfort else forclosed oure exyled eyes.

The two stanzas are not very coherent but they force our attention, they force us to consider the fugitives' plight and the contrasted perils of being hunted on land and drowned at sea. We have escaped from the abstract moralisings that are the norm of the *Mirror* to an imagined piece of real life.

There is another section that merits the kind of praise that Lewis gave Dolman's. It is the one immediately before, the story of Anthony Woodville, Lord Rivers and Scales, of unknown authorship. Coming as the first story in the additions of 1563, it marks the improved quality of some of these over the short and thin stories that composed the first issue of 1559. In the 1559 volume by far the longest section is that of the Duke of Clarence with 399 lines, but many of the sections run to less than a hundred. The average length of the 1563 stories is about 500 lines. This discrepancy between the 1559 volume and the 1563 additions is the stranger since there is evidence that several of the additions existed at the time when the first lot were collected. The reason may be that Baldwin, who edited both collections, did not wish to have his own thin substance put to shame by the

more weighty. In his revised dedication to the nobility in the
1563 volume[1] he stated that the additions contained "as
little of myne owne, as the fyrst part doth of other mens." He
knew the merit of Sackville's *Induction* and *Complaint of
Buckingham* and the probable popularity of Churchyard's
Jane Shore; and in order to have it both ways he held back
these and others so that both his own work would make the
greatest impact possible and the fame of the total collection
be enhanced by including ultimately the best work he had
been able to procure. This about Baldwin's motives is conjecture; but, whatever his motives, the story of Lord Rivers
is altogether ampler and more lively than anything printed
in 1559. The narrator's account of how Gloucester and
Buckingham trapped him at his inn at Northampton, where
he had remained because there was no room in the small
town of Stony Stratford, where the king lay, is not less vivid
than Hastings's account of being a fugitive at sea. Lord
Rivers and Scales recounts how his treacherous brother and
his accomplices come to his inn and congratulate him on his
good work in Wales, where he had suppressed some bandits.

> Fyrst to myne Inne, cummeth in my brother false,
> Embraceth me: wel met good brother Skales,
> And wepes withall: the other me enhalse
> With welcum coosyn, now welcum out of Wales,
> O happy day, for now all stormy gales
> Of stryfe and rancor utterly are swaged
> And we your owne to lyve or dye unwaged.

This verse captures the accent of true speech as nothing in
the 1559 volume had done. After a little homily on dissimu-
lation the narrator returns to real life with:

> They supped with me, propoundyng frendly talke
> Of our affayres, still gevyng me the prayse.
> And ever among the cups to mewarde walke:
> I drink to you good Cuz ech traytor sayes:
> Our banquet doen whan they should go theyr wayes
> They tooke theyr leave, oft wyshyng me good nyght
> As hartily as any creature myght.

[1] Ed. cit., p. 66.

The traitors inform the two dukes where Lord Rivers is lodging and during the night his servants tell him he has been betrayed.

> When I had opened the wyndow to look out
> There myght I see the streetes eche where beset,
> My inne on ech syde compassed about
> With armed watchmen, all escapes to let.

Easy in conscience, Lord Rivers cannot believe in the betrayal. He thinks that his house has been surrounded so that he shall not be the first to ride to Stratford to greet the king next morning.

> By thys the Dukes were cum into myne inne
> For they were lodged in another by.
> I gote me to them, thinkyng it a synne
> Within my chamber cowardly to lye.
> And meryly I asked my brother why
> He used me so? he sterne in evyll sadnes
> Cryed out: I arrest the traytor for thy badnes.

> How so (quoth I) whence ryseth your suspicion?
> Thou art a traytor (quoth he) I thee arrest.
> Arrest (quoth I) why where is your commission?
> He drew hys weapon, so dyd all the rest
> Crying: yeld the traytor. I so sor distrest
> Made no resystaunce: but was sent to ward
> None save theyr servauntes assygned to my gard.

Not only does the dialogue suggest real people talking but the author is genuinely possessed by his mental picture of the whole episode. He sees the inn and its surroundings; he has entered the mind of the victim. Sackville may write better poetry but he is farther from what he describes than is the anonymous author of Lord Rivers's complaint.

There are good things too in the complaint of the poet Collingbourne, executed by Richard III because of an indiscreet distich: namely the opening that bids poets beware tyrants and the passage describing the poet's office by likening him to Pegasus. In the opening the writer first complains that whatever the poet does is wrong:

> Be rough in ryme, and then they say you rayle,
> Though Juvenal so be, that makes no matter.

> Touche covertly in termes, and then you taunt,
> Though praysed Poetes, alway dyd the lyke.

And then he suddenly personates the overbearing ruler, who declares that he knows all about his own sins and fortune's wheel—in fact about the main doctrine and object of the *Mirror*—and that he needs no poet to inform him. Moreover, he holds the rudder and means to keep hold and has a good chance of escaping the punishment of his crimes. There is a humorous touch about the whole passage that looks forward to Harington's translation of Ariosto. The passage about the poet beginning, "The Greekes do paynt a Poetes office whole / In Pegasus," achieves a sustained eloquence culminating in these last two stanzas: a culmination which does not exclude the humorous lowering of tone in the final couplet and which is all the better for it:

> Like Pegasus a Poet must have wynges
> To flye to heaven, thereto to feed and reste:
> He must have knoweledge of eternal thynges,
> Almighty Iove must harber in his brest.
> With worldly cares he may not be opprest,
> The wynges of skyll and hope must heave him hyer,
> Than al the ioyes which worldy wyts desyre.

> He must be also nymble, free, and swyft
> To travayle farre to viewe the trades of men,
> Great knowledge oft is gotten by the shyft:
> Thynges notable he must be quicke to pen,
> Reprovyng vyces sharpely now and then.
> He must be swyft when touched tyrants chafe,
> To gallop thence to keep his carkas safe.

The complaint of Shore's Wife by Churchyard was throughout the sixteenth century one of the most admired sections of the *Mirror*. Modern opinion has been more hostile. Courthope,[1] for instance, contrasts the weight of Sackville with the emptiness of Churchyard. Possibly less

[1] W. J. Courthope, *A History of English Poetry*, 1897, ii, 126.

than justice has been done to Churchyard's smooth vacuity. After all, to be smooth and elegant in the reign of Edward VI was not a negligible achievement; and if you condemn all the poetry that says the same things in different ways you condemn a great deal. Here is a stanza, enlarging on Jane Shore's submission to the advances of Edward IV, which illustrates both the smoothness and the repetition.

> The Egles force, subdues eche byrd that flyes,
> What mettal may resist the flaming fyre?
> Doth not the sonne, dasill the clearest eyes,
> And melt the ise, and make the frost retire?
> Who can withstand a puissant kynges desyre?
> The stiffest stones are perced through with tooles,
> The wisest are with princes made but fooles.

This is perfect commonplace: the king-eagle-sun equation, the succession of well-worn sentiments. Yet it runs agreeably as did little contemporary verse. Churchyard can even convey feeling: the stanzas near the end describing Jane Shore's ultimate beggary remind one of Henryson's *Testament of Cresseid* in point of feeling as well as in point of substance:

> Where I was wont the golden chaynes to weare,
> A payre of beades about my necke was wound,
> A lynen clothe was lapt about my heare,
> A ragged gowne that trailed on the ground,
> A dishe that clapt and gave a heavie sound,
> A stayeng staffe and wallet therewithal,
> I bare about as witnesse of my fal.

> I had no house wherein to hide my head,
> The open strete my lodging was perforce,
> Ful ofte I went al hungry to my bed,
> My flesh consumed, I looked like a corse,
> Yet in that plyght who had on me remorse?
> O God thou knowest my frendes forsooke me than,
> Not one holpe me that suckered many a man.

Churchyard's *Cardinal Wolsey*, included in the final additions to the original *Mirror* in 1587 but almost certainly written much earlier (Wolsey's reference to Jane Shore as resembling himself for kindness in forwarding poor men's suits suggests that the two poems make a pair), has just the same qualities: the same smooth commonplace, the same capacity once in a way to feel a little and to lend a touch of distinction to his verse. In *Cardinal Wolsey* it is the account of Wolsey's state (ll. 134 ff.) that corresponds in quality to that of Jane Shore in her distress.

I cannot extend my plea for a kinder opinion of the poetry of the *Mirror* to the additions made by Higgins in 1574, 1575, and 1587 and by Blenerhasset in 1578. There are occasional pieces of crude vigour as in the account of Morindus in the belly of the monster that emerged from the Irish sea to afflict the north-west of Britain:

> The way was large, and downe he drew me in:
> A monstrous paunche for rowmthe and wondrous wide,
> But for I felte more softer there the skinne,
> At once I drewe, a dagger by my side:
> I knew my life, no longer could abide:
> For rammishe stenche, bloud, poyson, slymy glere:
> That in his body, so aboundant were.

But that is about all that can be said on their behalf as literature.

Turning from the aesthetic to the interesting I find the subject dividing itself naturally into two. First, there is the strange fact of the *Mirror's* persistent popularity, a fact rich in psychological interest. Second, there is the engaging sight of a group of men trying to work out literary problems among themselves and creating something which, whatever its deficiencies by modern standards, had the virtues of novelty and absolute integrity. I will enlarge on these two topics in turn.

There are many testimonies to the popularity of *A Mirror for Magistrates*, from the number and nature of the editions to Sidney's inclusion of it ("meetely furnished of beautiful parts") in his most select list of commendable English poems. But I know of no testimony so striking as that of Thomas Blenerhasset, whose additions to the *Mirror* the printer, Richard Webster, published in 1578 while the author, absent on garrison duty, was ignorant of the publication. After his own preface the printer placed a letter from Blenerhasset to the friend who had encouraged him in his presumptuous venture.[1] Blenerhasset, while aware of a gap in the series of laments that compose the *Mirror*, namely "from the conquest of Caesar unto the coming of Duke William the Conqueror," has no confidence about his own fitness to fill it. However, two of the Muses comfort him and he sees himself galloping (presumably in the form of Pegasus) through his possible rivals into the company of Sackville, Gascoigne,[2] and Churchyard, whose contributions he begs his friend to forget while reading his own. Blenerhasset then apologises for his deficiencies on the ground that in Guernsey, where he is serving, he has with him none of the chronicles which could serve as originals for the span of history he is concerned with and has to rely on his memory alone. Nor has he literary companions, "I sittyng on a Rocke in the Sea, not in *Spaine*, *Italie*, *Fraunce*, *Scotlande*, or *Englande*, but in *Garnzie* Castle, where although there be learned men, yet none which spende their tyme so vainely as in Poetrie." Not only does he lack copies of the chronicles but he has only four books with him: "the thirde Decade of Titus Livye, with *Boswelles Concordes of Armorie*, with *Monsignor de Lange*, that notable Warriour,[3] and with the unperfect *Mirrour for Magistrates*." What better testimony to the popularity of the *Mirror* than that a young officer going on lonely garrison duty should choose it as the one volume of poetry he allowed himself for his delectation?

And this popularity was long-lived as well as great. Only great popular support, well sustained, could have induced Baldwin, the *Mirror's* original editor, to continue to reissue and expand up to the year 1587 a volume ready for publica-

---

[1] *Parts added to "A Mirror for Magistrates" by John Higgins and Thomas Blenerhasset*, ed. Lily B. Campbell, 1946, pp. 379-83.

[2] The passage seems to me clearly to indicate that Blenerhasset looked on Gascoigne (or "Gascon" as he calls him) as a contributor to the *Mirror*. I know of no attempt to identify such a contribution.

[3] Miss Campbell (ed. cit., p. 368) identifies this as Guillaume du Bellay's *Instructions sur le faict de la guerre*, published in 1548 and frequently reissued.

tion, though not actually published, in 1555. And though the *Mirror* ceased to grow after 1587 (whether through Baldwin or Higgins or Blenerhasset), the literary mode it represented persisted well past the end of the century,[1] the latest example perhaps being Patrick Hannay's *Sheretine and Mariana*. This was published in 1622 and has been reprinted in the first volume of Saintsbury's *Caroline Poets*. It is unlike the *Mirror* in recounting a Hungarian not a British tragedy, but it is essentially like the *Mirror* in that the story is recounted in the first person by the ghost of Mariana.

Granted the popularity of the *Mirror*, what were the reasons for it? First, the political doctrines contained in it were, to the epoch its successive publications span, persistently living and present; and in two ways. The political theory is the perfect orthodoxy of the time. It is abundant and it covers most of the current, conventional, yet heart-felt opinions on kingship, obedience to authority, on the dividing-line between kingship and tyranny, on the sin of rebellion and the individual's ultimate responsibility, whatever the influence of the stars. Having written fairly fully on these matters[2] I will not pursue them here and I will go on to the second condition that made the political doctrine of the *Mirror* so living and hence so likely to be popular. And it is that the pattern of politics from 1555, when the *Mirror* should have seen its first publication (or even from a date in the reign of Edward VI, when at least one of the *Mirror's* sections was written), to 1587 was near enough to the pattern of politics from the reign of Richard II to that of Henry VIII to lend to the political misfortunes that are the subject of Baldwin's part of the *Mirror* a sense of actuality that it is most difficult for a modern reader to grasp. Students of history may grasp and give due weight to the changes that took place during Elizabeth's long reign; but by far the majority of readers or even students of literature allow the late years, between the Armada and the Essex rebellion, to stand for the whole of it.

[1] For this continuation see W. F. Trench, *A Mirror for Magistrates, its Origin and Influence*, 1898, pp. 81-3, 126 ff.

[2] In my *Shakespeare's History Plays*, 1945, pp. 71-90.

There was, of course, a very great deal more shedding of blood in the epoch in which the tragedies of the *Mirror* are set; yet the general political causes of danger and unrest are the same in both epochs. The succession was disputed, there were treason and revolt throughout all the years from the reign of Richard II to the accession of James I; and to think of the few, more settled, years after the Armada as representative is an error.

The first edition of the *Mirror* came out during the great hazards of Elizabeth's first year of rule. The second edition was contemporary with the momentous struggle between the Protestant and Catholic parties in Scotland. A little before the third edition (1571) came the actual Catholic rebellion in the north led by the Earls of Northumberland and Westmorland. A rebellious Percy had already provided a section of the *Mirror*, and the modern representative of the family would have provided a section with equal propriety. Thomas Percy, seventh Earl of Northumberland, was a main leader of the rebellions of 1569 and 1570. On their collapse he found asylum in Scotland and remained there two years. After much negotiation he was handed over to Elizabeth in 1572 and lost his head at York in August of that year. About two months before, there was executed in London a still more prominent nobleman after a career ideally suited to the norm of *A Mirror for Magistrates*. This was Thomas Howard, fourth Duke of Norfolk, the most eminent and the richest noblemen in England. He was not a declared Catholic but he was not at all averse to becoming one if this should profit him. He was greatly ambitious, for he aspired to marrying Mary of Scotland. When he found that Elizabeth disapproved and blocked his way, he drifted into treason and covertly supported the Spaniard, Ridolfi, who was fostering a possible invasion of England. The Duke's treason was discovered and he was beheaded on Tower Hill. With such apt repetitions of the subject-matter of the *Mirror* how could its substance fail to live?

In the year of the second rebellion Elizabeth was excommunicated, and the Jesuits began their infiltration. The next year a new homily, *Against Disobedience and Wilful Rebellion*, was added to the existing collection. Its sentiments were in perfect harmony with those of *A Mirror for Magistrates*. In the year when the two earls were executed occurred the St Bartholomew Massacre, the Dutch revolt against Spain, and the first of the Commons' petitions for the death of Mary. Uncertainty of the future, fear, and suspicion prevailed in England between the beginning of Queen Mary's captivity and her death in 1587. During that span there were three reissues of the *Mirror*; and in the year of Mary's execution, after the discovery of Babington's plot, the last additions (two of them, strangely enough, dealing with Scotland) were made to Baldwin's section of the *Mirror*. In fact, throughout the years when Baldwin's *Mirror* was being created, history re-enacted the main themes of its political morality.

A second reason for the *Mirror's* popularity was that it provided through the trappings of the poetical rhetoric of the day a portion of those matters of history and legend with which many Elizabethans wished to be familiar. It is a reason that applies equally to Baldwin's *Mirror* and to the additions of Higgins and Blenerhasset. These additions lack the political earnestness of the original *Mirror* but they are highly informative on the legends and history which, deriving from Geoffrey of Monmouth as well as from more trustworthy sources, were part of the living commonplaces of the age of Elizabeth.

The modern reader is apt to ask: why, when the Elizabethans could get these commonplaces through the tolerable prose of the chronicles, did they insist on getting it also through the execrable verse of Warner or Higgins or Blenerhasset?; how came it that Meres could have "heard him [Warner] termd of the best wits of both our Universities our English Homer" when those best wits could have got the substance of *Albion's England* in harmless prose elsewhere? The answer is that certain poems, however alien to modern taste and however poor as poetry by enduring standards, mediated their information through a rhetoric which the Elizabethans found highly entertaining. I will give two types of illustration.

First, the very form of the soliloquy, in which the tragedies of the *Mirror* were cast, was for the Elizabethans more live and dramatic than for us. Characters in the medieval drama were often informative about themselves and their doings; and this habit left its legacy to the succeeding age. Readers of the *Mirror* would have enjoyed picturing the ghosts of the characters returning from the dead and addressing Baldwin and his fellows. Their enjoyment was increased by the help Baldwin himself on many occasions (and Sackville on a single occasion) gave to the process of dramatising. Constantly in the end-links Baldwin introduces a new story by asking us to picture the teller. Before the complaint of James IV of Scotland he wrote: "Thinke then (quoth I) that you see him standing all wounded, with a shafte in his body, and emongst other woundes, one geven by a byll, both deadly, to say in his rude and faithlesse manner as followeth." The author of the complaint of Richard II is made to say in the preceding end-link: "And therefore imagine *Baldwin* that you see him al to be mangled, with blew woundes, lying pale and wanne al naked upon the cold stones in Paules church, the people standing round, about him, and making his mone in this sort." More elaborate is the introduction of the poet Collingbourne:

> I have his Tragedie here (quoth I) For the better perceyving whereof, you must ymagin that you se him a mervaylous wel favoured man, holding in his hand his owne hart, newely ripped out of his brest, and smoking forth the lively spirit: and with his other hand, beckening to and fro, as it were to warne us to avoyde: and with his faynte tounge and voyce, sayeing as coragiously as he may, these wordes that follow.

There is no prose end-link before Sackville's tragedy of Buckingham, there being the same author's induction in verse. But he is careful to heighten the drama by devoting the last three stanzas of his induction to a melodramatic description of Buckingham's appearance as he tells his tale. Most elaborate of all is Baldwin's preface to the tragedy of Richard Duke of York, killed at the Battle of Wakefield. Here, exceptionally, Baldwin adopts the dream technique and has this vision:

Me thought there stode before us, a tall mans body full of fresshe woundes, but lackyng a head, holdyng by the hande a goodlye childe, whose brest was so wounded that his hearte myght be seen, his lovely face and eyes disfigured with dropping teares, his heare through horrour standyng upryght, his mercy cravyng handes all to bemangled, and all his body embrued with his own bloud. And whan through the gastfulnes of this pyteous spectacle, I waxed afeard, and turned away my face, me thought there came a shrekyng voyce out of the weasande pipe of the headles bodye, saying as foloweth.

I have to admit that in reading the *Mirror* I simply cannot induce my imagination to take such pictures seriously or use them to animate the stories that follow; and I doubt if others today have succeeded better. But I am sure that the case was different in the sixteenth century and that this dramatic staging of the tragedies was one reason why *A Mirror for Magistrates* was so widely read.

My second type of illustration has to do with the way some of the tragedies in the *Mirror* amplify and embellish the stories found in the chronicles. I will give examples from Higgins's portion of the *Mirror*.

Among the tragedies in Higgins's first issue, in 1574, is that of Bladud, one of the earliest kings of Britain. His legend goes back to Geoffrey of Monmouth, who briefly informs us that he built Kaerbadus or Bath and made hot baths for the benefit of the public. Later he turned to magic, tried to fly, and suffered the fate of Icarus. Fabyan and Holinshed are brief on Bladud, adding little to Geoffrey. But Grafton has the further story of Bladud's going to the University of Athens to be educated, of his bringing back philosophers to Britain, and of his founding a university at Stamford. Higgins turned Grafton's fuller account into 316 lines of crude but speedy ballad-metre. Repenting of this metre, he told the same story in abbreviated form in his second edition, 1587, using rime royal. It is the first version that should make us see why narrative in poor verse could compete with narrative in tolerable prose. Though Higgins writes crudely, he infuses some kind of life into his story by the wealth of detail he adds. He gives Prince Bladud a thoroughly traditional education at Athens in the Trivium and Quadrivium, going into precise details; and anticipates his later disasters by having him taught the rudiments of magic at the same place. A further embellishment is that Bladud had a great reception when he returned to Britain:

> I was receavd with triumphes great,
> With pageauntes in eache towne I paste:
> And at the courte my princly seate,
> Was by my fathers ioyned faste.

> The nobles then desirde to have
> On me their children wayte and tend:
> And royall giftes with them me gave,
> As might their powres therto extende.

The four philosophers he brought from Greece were at great pains to find the right site; and in the end find Stamford

> With water streames, and springes for welles;
> And medowes sweete, and valeyes grene:
> And woodes, groaves, quaries, all thinge else
> For studentes weale, or pleasure bene.

The chroniclers had not troubled to remind us that there is Ketton and Barnack stone near Stamford. Higgins is even ampler in his mustering all the diseases which the waters of Bladud's newly founded spa could cure; and after the list he makes Bladud break out into rhetoric:

> Shall I renege I made them then?
> Shall I denye my cunning founde,
> By helpe I had of learned men,
> Those worthy welles in gratefull grounde?

If, as I do, I find Higgins's account of Bladud more diverting than the account in the chronicles, an Elizabethan is likely to have found it so in a still higher degree.

Or take the next story in Higgins's first series, that of Cordila. It runs to 371 lines and in its account of Cordila's suicide in prison is far more detailed and embroidered than anything in the chronicles. She laments her lot in strict accord with what contemporary notions of rhetoric demanded:

Was ever lady in such wofull wreckfull wo:
Deprivde of princely powre, berefte of libertie,
Deprivd in all these worldly pompes, hir pleasures fro,
And brought from welthe, to nede distresse, and misery?
From palace proude, in prison poore to lye:
From kingdomes twayne, to dungion one no more:
From Ladies wayting, unto vermine store.

And so on, with a lot more *from's* and *to's*. Nor does she merely take her life. Instead, she is persuaded to do so by a "gryzely ghost" called "Despayre," who tells her she will never regain her kingdom and offers her a fine selection of the means of destruction: "knyves, sharpe swordes, poynadoes all bedyde with bloud, and poysons." In view of all this rhetoric and melodrama, so perfectly in the prevailing fashion, we need not now be shocked, as most of our fathers would have been, at the strong evidence in favour of Shakespeare's familiarity with the Cordelia story in the *Mirror* and indeed with the whole book, its worst parts included.[1] Born in 1564, Shakespeare was just of an age to be subject to the popularity of the enlarged issues of the *Mirror* in 1574 and 1587. Despair offering her instruments of self-destruction to Cordila was the perfect aliment for the digestion of the adolescent reader of the day. Nothing in the chronicles was so nicely suited.

In sum, there are pretty good reasons for the *Mirror's* popularity in its own day.

I said that the dramatic stage-directions of the end-links made little impression on me but I did not mean thereby to imply that these end-links are negligible. On the contrary I believe that for modern readers they supply the best means of bringing *A Mirror for Magistrates* to life. Indeed they gain from a distant view and are worth more to us than to the readers at whom they were aimed. They make a piece of history more living than the literature to which they are appended. Their great virtues are of being intimate and

[1] See Kenneth Muir, *Shakespeare's Sources*, vol. i, 1957, especially p. 143, and Harold F. Brooks, Appendix A, pp. 212-16, of J. M. Nosworthy's (Arden) edition of *Cymbeline*, 1955.

authentic. And through those virtues they give a fascinating glimpse of a group of rising young men working out their problems of literary creation.

Of the intimacy there is no doubt. Baldwin's end-links tell of the thoughts and aims of a group of friends. The authenticity is different. The accounts given of the genesis of the poem cannot be literally true: for too much is crowded into a single session of friends to admit the reality of actual life. For instance, in the opening account contained in *William Baldwin to the Reader* everything happens at once. The seven men who have assembled discuss how to continue Lydgate's translation of Boccaccio. They will personate "wretched princes" and make their moan to Baldwin, the editor. They consult the chronicles for finding fit subjects, and Ferrers proposes that they should concentrate on English unfortunates who lived after the date of Boccaccio's most recent characters. So the stories of Richard I and King John, though excellent material, must be excluded, because the printer wants the time-sequence preserved, and these kings come too early. Ferrers then passes from theory to practice and recounts the story of Chief Justice Tresilian, who came to an evil end in the reign of Richard II. Now, though things cannot have happened just like that, there is not the least doubt that at one time or another they did happen. What we have is a number of true events which occurred at several different times telescoped into a single session. This telescoping is a trivial distortion of the truth; and the authenticity remains paramount.

Exactly the same mixture of authenticity and telescoping marks Baldwin's address to the reader in his second, 1563, edition. He recounts how he and the printer and all his helpers except Ferrers met together. After a little Ferrers enters, is blamed for his lateness, and apologises for it on the plea that he has been collecting tragedies from his friends and that all but a few have let him down because they are so slow:

for sum wyttes are readye, and dispatch many matters spedilye, lyke the Conye which lyttereth every moneth: sum other are slowe lyke the Olyfaunt, skarce delyveryng any matter in ten

yeares. I disprayse nether of these byrthes, for both be naturall:
But I commende most the meane, which is neyther to slow nor to
swyft, for that is Lion lyke, and therefore most noble. For the
ryght poet doth neyther through haste bring furth swift feble
Rabettes, neither doth he weary men in lookyng for hys strong
joyntles Olyphantes: But in reasonable tyme he bryngeth furth a
perfect and lively Lion, not a Bearwhelp that must be longar in
lyckyng than in breedynge.

Ferrers goes on to say what tragedies he has procured; the
printer and Baldwin do the same; and the company settle to
hear them read aloud. Plainly, the scene is largely fictitious.
It is unthinkable that Ferrers waited till the day appointed
for meeting and reading the new material before collecting
his friends' contributions. Nor is it the least conceivable that
all the new matter was read during a single session. Again,
several visits, several meetings and readings, have been
telescoped. And again this telescoping counts for nothing,
while the authenticity counts for a great deal. We are given a
glimpse of real meetings to discuss the composition of the
volume and to hear the contributions read aloud. I do not
doubt that the talk about rabbits and elephants is genuine
talk, especially because the rabbits crop up again in a later
end-link, making one surmise that they were a stock joke in
the company.

Apart from this general authenticity there is the pleasure
of seeing the group interested in the details of their craft; and
here the end-links join with the great amount of metrical
experiment that occurs throughout the whole length of the
Mirror. This reinforces very powerfully the impression that
in the Mirror we have the spectacle of a group of men feeling
their way towards the right literary procedure. Alwin Thaler[1]
has written on the literary criticism of the Mirror; but in
truth it amounts in itself to little. The company discuss, for
instance, the principle of decorum, but they do not carry the
topic farther than the need to make the kind of metre suit the
kind of speaker. For instance, the end-link after the story of
the Blacksmith begins:

[1] See J.E.G.P., 1950, xlix. 1-13.

It is pitie (quoth one) that the meter is no better seing that the matter is so good: you maye doo verye well to helpe it, and a littell fylyng would make it formall. The Author him selfe (quoth I) could have doen that, but he woulde not, and hath desyred me that it maye passe in such rude sort as you have heard it: for he observeth therein a double *decorum* both of the Smith, and of him selfe: for he thinketh it not mete for the Smyth to speke, nor for himselfe to write in any exacte kynde of meter.

That is all very well, but no one of the company observes that the tale itself is full of high sentiments perfectly inappropriate to the character of the speaker and to the intentional roughness of the metre, including an eloquent plea that the nobility should be properly educated. Actually the same observation had been made after Jack Cade told his story:

> By saint mary (quoth one) yf Iacke wer as well learned, as you have made his oracion, What so ever he was by byrth, I warrant him a gentylman by his learnyng. How notably and Philosopher like hath he discrybed Fortune and the causes of worldly cumbraunce? howe upryghtly also and howe like a devine hath he determined the states both of officers and Rebelles.

But no one takes up this satirical comment. No, it is not the criticism in itself that matters but the fresh and genuine picture that the *Mirror* provides of real people airing their opinions. They are genuinely concerned with the questions of why the chronicles are so often at variance with one another, whether the fat prior of Tiptree, who was squeezed to death in the throng on London Bridge, could furnish an edifying tale, whether good Protestants may introduce the Popish creation of Purgatory into their verses, what freedom the poet may be allowed, whether women may be learned. We may be absolutely assured that this eager group of people discussed these topics; and it is this assurance that gives to *A Mirror for Magistrates* its main attraction for the reader of today.

II EDUCATIONAL

Two Ways of Learning

T H E two volumes under consideration[1] are the first pair of a new series of anthologies of English literature covering the centuries from the sixteenth to the nineteenth but omitting the drama. They preserve the original spelling with scrupulous academic care; they are prefaced by short but informative essays; and the texts are provided with a glossary at the foot of the page. The editors have done all they can to direct attention to the texts and to make them understandable to the reader. They have also taken a great deal of trouble over their choice of texts. While not excluding things that have been anthologised before, they have sought to include much new matter; and on the whole they have compromised very well. They adopted a wrong principle when they included things so easily accessible elsewhere as parts of *Venus and Adonis* and Sidney's *Apologie for Poetry* instead of leaving room for more unanthologised matter; but, granted that principle, both anthologies bear the marks of long and sensible thought and of much hard work.

Of course no one can fail to find fault with any anthology other than his own; and in considering the verse selection it may be asked why Dunbar should be represented by only the "Goldyn Targe" and the "Lament for the Makaris" without any of the satirical pieces, why none of Douglas's poetical prologues to his translation of the *Aeneid* is included, why Sidney should get fewer pages than Fulke Greville, and why Sir John Davies should be represented by *Nosce Teipsum* alone, unseconded by the airiness of *Orchestra*. Then, in the prose, North's *Plutarch* shows up poorly in snippets and would have been better represented by a single complete life, while Hall and Puttenham have not been treated with sufficient generosity. But it is much easier for a reviewer to carp in this style than it was for the editors to score their

[1] Karl J. Holzknecht (Editor): *Sixteenth-Century English Prose*. Norman E. McClure (Editor): *Sixteenth-Century English Poetry*.

conspicuous successes in the anthological art. One of these is to have extracted from Gascoigne's *Adventures of Master F. J.* the little tale told by the Lady Frances about the successful patience of an abused husband, and to have followed it by Pettie's story of Admetus and Alcest. Neither piece is well known, and one supplements the other charmingly. Gascoigne, for an Elizabethan, writes simply and tersely and holds the reader through the interest of the story in itself. Pettie's prose is florid, like Lyly's, and charms by the vitality with which it draws attention to itself. Some of the extracts from the lesson-books for language teaching are most diverting; and one of those from John Eliot's *Ortho-epia Gallica*, an imaginary dialogue between a passenger and a sailor on a Channel crossing, sounds in part like an anticipatory parody of the first scene of the *Tempest*:

> *Sailor*. It thundreth, it lightneth, it raineth, it haileth; it is best to strike saile and to vire the cables. To the deck ho: to the Sterne: This waue will carrie vs to all the Diuels.
>
> *Passenger*. O God the Sauiour. O my friends: O thrice and foure times happie are those who are on firme land setting of beanes. . . . O God we are now at the bottome of the sea. I giue eighteen hundred thousand crownes of reuenue to him who will set me a land.

In the verse anthology, the four versified Psalms of Sternhold that are included will surprise many readers by being so much better poetically than Sternhold's reputation would lead them to expect. And, granted that Spenser should be included at all in the anthology, it was a happy thought to represent the *Faerie Queene* by the Mutability Cantos alone, detached as they are already from the body of the poem. And, against the complaint that Davies should have been represented by more than one kind of his verse, it is impossible to see how the selection from Daniel could be better: a selection admirably balanced and showing that the anthologist is thoroughly and sensitively acquainted with the whole range of Daniel's work. On a balance, then, these two anthologies are in their kind very good indeed.

But what of that kind? That question points to a problem

of education; and perhaps a reviewer may pursue that problem instead of taking the more obvious course and asking what light these twin anthologies throw on the comparative achievement of poets and prose writers in the sixteenth century.

In bulk these are formidable volumes; they contain a very large area of print. To accommodate the maximum of this the prose is printed in double columns; and so is the verse, where the lines are short enough. Most of the verse does indeed get the benefit of the single column on the page; but the fragile delicacy of Wyatt's "What shulde I saye?" is subjected to the indignity of the double column. Granted this need for compression, the production is good and the printer has done his best to make his material presentable. But in spite of his efforts the two volumes are very evidently designed for a practical end as prescribed texts at American universities. They are meant for large classes in English literature, where chunks from them will be set, from lesson to lesson, as assignments. Now Professor McClure says in his preface, "It is hoped that many who use this book will continue their reading and study in the original texts and standard editions"; and we may applaud the sentiment: but we shall find it difficult not to criticise the volumes for suggesting by their very form and nature that here is all you need to know about the sixteenth century. Good as the anthologies are, it is difficult to suppress the temptation to look on them as a kind of reader's digest. But this may be a prejudiced view and we should try to consider dispassionately the cases for and against this sort of volume.

One of the drawbacks of the ordinary university lecture on a general literary topic is that it is too much in the air. The lecturer may try to remain concrete by quoting, but that is a different matter from the listeners having the texts before them and being able to read for themselves any passage to which the lecturer refers. If every man in the audience has his text, and the lecturer in his discourse does not go outside that text, there is a good chance that the brighter and more curious members of the audience may punctuate the lecture by questions. But, above all, with anthologies such as these for basis, there is every inducement for the lecturer to be concrete, to talk on the text rather than about the text, to arrive at the general through the particular. And though at its worst this method may end in a dreary and blinkered ingenuity it remains the right method and immeasurably better than the older fashion of entering literature through the supposed facts of literary history.

Secondly, if a large number of students use the same anthology, they may acquire some kind of cultural kinship in a world where such kinship grows ever rarer. A strength of eighteenth-century education was its limits and its uniformity. All educated men knew their Horace. Now, many highly educated men simply do not speak each other's cultural language; and the cultural case of the modern world is more like that of the post-classical world when the legacy of Asia was added to that of Greece and Rome. There was too much to cope with, and the only hope was to jettison and anthologise. In a long view the impulse behind such anthologies as are now under review and the encyclopedias of Isidore of Seville may be the same. Be this as it may, in an age when Shakespeare but very little else is still common property, there is something to be said for rigidity, for making undergraduates read the same things. A good teacher may impress on a big group of men a common realisation that certain pieces of literature are memorable; and that will constitute a bond in a disintegrating culture.

Nevertheless, the case against this kind of anthology is formidable. Their very virtues, their amplitude and inclusiveness, are likely to have the wrong effect. Where there is such wealth, what inducement is there to go outside the prescribed matter? And when such inducement is lacking, the undergraduate is all too apt to conclude that other kinds of initiative are not required. If his teachers have prescribed exactly what he ought to read, why should they not go further and tell him what he has got to think? And if he can memorise what he has been told, has he not done all that can be required of him? In a way it is a mistake for anthologies to be too good. One of their functions is to constitute a challenge. If an anthologist causes a reader to exclaim indignantly, "Oh, he hasn't included *x*: what a shame," and then to re-read *x* to confirm or invalidate his indignation, he has fulfilled part of his function. But a class reading a prescribed anthology will be all too apt to assume that it must not be challenged, that unassailable authority has imposed it.

That there should in every age be some kind of accepted anthology of masterpieces is desirable. It will, of course, change from age to age, but in its own age it will be a bond between educated people. It should not, however, be large, and it should consist only of what people at that time have agreed to think of the first excellence; it will in fact contain those things which it is a disgrace not to have read. When the series of which the two present volumes form part is complete, it will contain nearly 5,000 packed pages: a great deal more than any undergraduate could genuinely assimilate during his university course. Indeed any attempt to do so could only result in hopeless confusion of mind, through a desperate and unreflecting exercise of the bare memory. The right general principle is surely this: the farther the student gets away from the things it is a disgrace for him not to have read, the more choice he should be allowed to follow his own tastes. There is a genuine social reason for reading the masterpieces that takes the sting out of the compulsion to read them, but this reason is not valid for the secondary works.

The point can be made clearer by an example taken from Professor McClure's volume. He includes, as he was bound to do, that immensely popular, and many times added to, collection of tragic narratives, *A Mirror for Magistrates*. And, very properly, he does not confine his selection to the best-known thing in the book, Sackville's *Induction*. More properly still he does not print the *Induction* first as if it were the introduction to the whole series of tales and not, as in fact it is, the introduction to the *Complaynt of Henrye Duke of Buckingham*, also the work of Sackville. Instead, he puts before it the story of Jack Cade from the original version of the *Mirror* and after it the story of Wolsey, added in a later edition. The two stories are well chosen because they point to the great metrical variety of the *Mirror* as a whole. Jack

Cade speaks in cadences remote from the regular iambic line
that was to dominate rather later in the century:

> Shal I cal it Fortune or my froward folly
> That lifted me, and layed me downe below?
> Or was it courage that me made so Ioly,
> Which of the starres and bodyes grement grow?

Contrast this with the regularity of Wolsey's:

> I ioyde to see my seruantes thriue so well,
> And go so gay, with little that they gote:
> For as I did in honour still excell,
> So would I oft the wante of seruantes note.

And the anthologist even includes in a note part of the end-
link that follows Cade's tragedy, thus giving a sample of one
of the things that most give the *Mirror* its interest. Granted
his limits, the anthologist could not have done much better.

But what of the effect of such a selection on the student of
English at a university? He is likely to find the roughness of
Jack Cade repellent; and indeed as poetry Jack Cade's story
has no merit. He is likely to get some kind of pleasure from
Sackville's stately gloom—

> And first within the portche and iawes of Hell
> Sate diepe Remorse of conscience, al besprent
> With teares—

but to end by thinking that this particular mode is kept up
too long. And he is likely to tolerate the competent but not
exhilarating narrative of Wolsey. Most of what he will take
away with him for permanent enjoyment could be com-
pressed into a selection of some of the best stanzas from the
Induction. It is doubtful if the virtues of Professor McClure's
selection, to which tribute has been paid, would in fact
induce the student to benefit from the things that the *Mirror*
has most to offer. Of course, not many students ever will,
under any conditions. Why should they, when there is so
much else to read? And yet it is possible to imagine an
occasional student, especially one bred in a place where
assignments are few and options wide, curious perhaps to see

in what context the stanzas from the *Induction* occurred, or to sample a book that obviously meant so much to the Elizabethans, going to the library and trying to get a notion of what the whole thing was like. And one can imagine him, if he read consecutively for some while, and took the end-links as integral parts of the whole, beginning to see that he was reading an experimental work, a work not of the first literary merit yet interesting and even fascinating because it shows a process of growth, of a new exploration in a period when the poetic impulse was at an ebb. The authors of the first published edition of the *Mirror* were a group of friends who, in adopting the old theme of Lydgate on the fall of great men, wanted to make something new and were as yet uncertain how they should do it. All sorts of problems confront them, metrical, political, ethical; and it is just because the answers are in dispute that the *Mirror*, though mediocre as poetry, is yet thoroughly alive. And the man who tackles the *Mirror* as a whole rather than samples it in an anthology, however good, is the one who is most likely to detect and to enjoy the thing that the poem has most to offer.

The problem raised is the old one of the comparative claims of restricted excellence and widespread mediocrity. The two anthologies under review will certainly succeed in serving the second; they can hardly expect, however good their intentions, to serve both.

Research in the Humanities

IT was with some reluctance that I accepted an invitation of the Humanities Research Council of Canada to speak to various Canadian universities on research; and for some very good reasons. First, I regard myself more as a general practitioner of academic criticism than as a strict researcher; the only time when I was the latter being a couple of postgraduate years when I gained some expert knowledge of certain wares of Greek pottery. Secondly, I believe undergraduate teaching more important than graduate teaching. And lastly I am critical of certain recent trends in research and cannot refrain from attacking them. For all these reasons I risked appearing to sabotage the very things I was asked to promote. This risk I must deal with at the outset; and therefore I begin by affirming that in spite of abuses the act of research is founded safely on certain permanent human instincts.

The simplest of these instincts (and the only one I shall refer to) is that of curiosity, of that desire to learn, which Aristotle said was something deep down in human nature. Any man in whom that instinct is faint or dormant is incomplete. Milton in *Paradise Lost* made it very prominent in Adam, first by saying that he was formed for contemplation as well as for valour and second by making him question Raphael on the facts of the universe with evident curiosity. Adam in Book Seven asked Raphael:

> what cause
> Mov'd the Creator, in his holy rest
> Through all eternity, so late to build
> In Chaos, and the work begun how soon
> Absolv'd; if unforbid thou mayst unfold
> What we, not to explore the secrets ask
> Of his eternal empire but the more
> To magnify his work, the more we know.

And the great light of day yet wants to run
Much of his race through steep; suspense in Heav'n
Held by thy voice, thy potent voice he hears,
And longer will delay to hear thee tell
His generation.

Adam is eager for knowledge and he imagines the sun as eager
as himself, oblivious of time. Milton did well to add that touch
about the sun, for it affirms the genuineness of the curiosity;
and the oblivious scholar, although not the complete man,
embodies that powerful instinct for knowledge which the
complete man ought among other qualities to possess.

Now though this instinct of curiosity is a good thing in
itself, it cannot be finally evaluated in isolation. It can be a
good servant of life but when it becomes master it can be
vicious and a danger to a proper human balance. Milton,
living in a theological age and writing a theological poem,
put this sentiment in terms of God, as the above passage
illustrates. Adam, though filled with the simple instinct of
human curiosity, subordinates it to the glory of God. He
disclaims the desire to know God's secrets; and he wants to
know all things permissible only in order to magnify God the
more. It is no new doctrine in Milton, and he can put it in
less theological terms. In his letter to an anonymous friend
in the Trinity Manuscript he discusses the "mere love of
learning" and its uses and abuses. In its bad form it is "a
poor regardless and unprofitable sin of curiosity . . . whereby
a man cuts himself off from all action and becomes the most
helpless, pusillanimous, and unweaponed creature in the
world, the most unfit and unable to do that which all mortals
aspire to." And between this letter and *Paradise Lost* comes
the tract *Of Education*, where Milton's paramount premiss
is that learning must subserve the total interests of man. Its
object is the knowledge of God, which is very different from
the mere accumulation of facts and which can make a man of
little book learning but of a balanced judgement better than
an ill-balanced sciolist:

And though a linguist should pride himself to have all the tongues
that Babel cleft the world into, yet if he have not studied the solid

things in them as well as the words and lexicons, he were nothing
so much to be esteemed a worthy man as any yeoman or tradesman
competently wise in his mother dialect only.

And though Milton would have put it otherwise he would
have agreed that the health of research must depend on its
ministering to the general good of mankind.

Now that is a highly contentious statement, because it
goes against the creed of much scientific research that there
exists a goddess called Truth and that any extension of her
empire is self-valuable apart from all human considerations.
Now,

> Had we but world enough and time,
> Such creed, researcher, were no crime;

but it is madness not to hear Time's winged chariot at our
back and not to adapt our creed to the limiting conditions of
our life. What is the use of an unceasing extension of Truth
that causes a man to forget his humanity? In the relative
considerations of life as it actually exists there is little comfort in those lines of Clough that sum up so well the stern
scientific creed:

> It fortifies my soul to know
> That, though I perish, Truth is so.

This mistaken erection of Truth into a goddess is due to a
confusion of doctrines. The right doctrine of scientific truth
is: not to flinch at the facts, or, in Keats's phrase, "to bear all
naked truth." The false doctrine is that there is no hierarchy
of truths according to their value in human life. And it
cannot be said too often that not Truth but those truths that
serve the good of man is what should be the concern of
humane research.

Reinforcing the cult of Truth as an incentive to any sort of
research is an urge that operates quite outside the province
of learning: the urge to produce. It is a sinister fact of the
modern world that the sheer urge to produce is habitually
put above human needs: in particular that the *rationale* of
much industry is not, *how can we serve genuine and justified*

human needs? but, *how can we plant on a bewildered public the things it's the best fun or the easiest task for us to produce?* In other words the producer indulges his own pride at the expense of the human beings he is supposed to be serving.

This publication for publication's sake, or more often for the sake of getting academic promotion, is a very serious matter indeed, leading to a monstrous inflation of print and apt to bring all learning into disrepute. I sometimes think that the crude and brutal anti-intellectualism of the Nazi movement was partly due to the excesses of German academic production; to that soulless grinding out of mechanical theses that obscured the genuine nobility of a proportion of German scholarship. And I fear that if there is not some strong counter-movement in favour of quality against quantity Germany will not have been the only country where at one time so-called scholarship has proved the worst enemy of things of the mind.

At this point you may well ask me if I have any antidotes to offer against this great production-drive in research. And I answer that I never would have been so Jeremiac gratuitously. Indeed it is about these very antidotes that I wish to speak with most emphasis. I begin with the most simple and practical.

These simple remedies (by which I mean *simple in themselves*, not *easily applied*, for the forces making against their application are very powerful) fall into two rough classes that I can label elective and editorial. Under the elective heading I advance the remedial principle that for academic appointment and promotion nothing beyond efficiency or eminence as a teacher is required. In actual fact, most efficient or eminent teachers will *want* to do some writing, and are likely to suffer in efficiency if they do not indulge that want. But there exist also people who have not that want and are, as teachers, quite the equals of those who have it; and they should neither be denied promotion nor forced to do research against the grain. There is an admirable passage in Irving Babbitt's *Literature and the American College* where he attacks Münsterberg's assertion that there are only two kinds of scholar, the productive and the receptive: those who discover knowledge and those who receive, or having received, distribute it. Babbitt points out that Münsterberg has omitted the most important principle of all: that of reflection. And he speaks of

> that human endeavour which it is the special purpose of the college to foster—that effort of reflection, virile above all others, to co-ordinate the scattered elements of knowledge, and relate them not only to the intellect but to the will and character; that subtle alchemy by which mere learning is transmuted into culture.

A teacher who reflects, who himself fulfils this co-ordinating task and teaches others to do the same, though publishing nothing, is far more worthy of a professorial chair than another who has amassed a stack of unreflective compilation. Think of the case of Epictetus. He was a professor of philosophy in the ancient world and he lectured but never published. His main works have been preserved for us through the lecture-notes of his pupils. It is a sobering thought that Epictetus would have lost his job today in the University of ——; well, I had better leave it to you to supply, as you think fit, the missing word or words.

Secondly, on the elective side, it is essential that electors, when, as they properly should, they review published work of candidates, give weight to quality and not quantity. That sense of assurance given to electing bodies by so many square yards of print is a terrible snare. You know the kind of thing that can happen. So many dossiers of candidates circulated; lists of published work; coming at a hot and busy time of the year; most of the published work not known to the electors, only known of; hasty visits to the library to become better acquainted with it; a suspicion that A, who hasn't published much, is rather able, but his stuff is concentrated and needs re-reading and there isn't time, and you're not certain if he's really good after all; B and C are straightforward and pro- ductive—you know where you are with them, and they know where they are with you, for their bibliographies make a fine showing—and the job goes to B or C. Possibly it *should* go to B or C; but there will be similar cases when A will be head and shoulders above them in quality and not get the job. That is what *can* happen; and in this fallible world it always will happen sometimes. My point is that the less often it happens, the greater will be the inducement to men to do reflective and not mechanical research, to cut down quantity and aim at quality.

Turn now to the editorial side; and by that I mean any criticism by editor or reviewer or reading public that can influence the bulk or character of published research work. I know little of the workings of the learned periodicals, but I believe their editors to be devoted men, fulfilling their duties in addition to other (and main) duties, gaining no or little money reward and earning far less thanks than is their due. Some may be able to exercise a drastic critical control of the matter submitted to them; others may have no time or strength beyond the mere act of acceptance or rejection. Anyhow, it is true that many of the articles that get printed are far longer than they should be: not really articles at all but inflated notes. Similarly, many books are merely inflated articles. The bulk of research could be reduced, and its effectiveness in almost inverse proportion increased, by a much greater editorial severity. In fact the general standard of acceptance for publication should be very greatly raised. Reviewers and reading public could back up editorial severity by unqualified apportionment of proper praise and blame.

These, then are the remedies, simple to set forth but all too difficult to apply, for the characteristic abuses of the practice of research. The last mentioned remedy, editorial severity, might also do much to cure one of the ills that must bring research into disrepute while hindering its efficacy; namely graceless and obscure writing. Before trying to read a recent book of scholarship I read reviews of it and talked to some highly competent readers of it. Reviews and readers agreed that the substance was interesting and important but that the style made the process of grasping that substance a burden. Coming to the book myself, I was struck first by the real erudition and the distinguished mental equipment of the writer and next by his total disregard of the common reader's convenience. Though again and again showing himself capable of witty and felicitous phrases, he frequently wrote sentences of appalling ugliness needing three or four readings to be understood. Moreover he appeared to assume an equipment in the reader nearly as formidable as his own. The book runs to 425 pages. I reckon it would take me about three month's uninterrupted study to read and grasp it from end to end. Certainly I should be much wiser after those three months study. But what of all the other books—shorter and more lucid—I might have read in the time? I shall probably content myself with a general idea of the book's position based on cursory glances and the reports of others. And I cannot see the common educated reader doing much more than this. And the book is but one of a number of books or articles which have neglected or disclaimed the elementary obligation of the author to consult the interests of the reader, to perform that social act of grace and intelligibility that no writer of the eighteenth century ever dreamed you could omit. It seems to me a terrible thing that research work that purports to be humane and to deal with matters of culture should by its manner of writing flout the very things it professes to promote.

So much for practical remedies for some of our present ills. I go on to a general principle essential for keeping research healthy; but I shall apply it only to research that touches works of art. And the principle is that such research can only be justified when it subserves the ultimate exercise of the aesthetic critical faculty; which is merely to put more specially the larger doctrine that learning must minister to the general good of man. And please remember that from now on I am speaking of what relates to *imaginative* writing and not to antiquarianism, or the history of ideas as such, or social life. Much research in English Faculties belongs to these other classes, and if it is content to do so can be justified by other relations than one with the aesthetic critical faculty.

It may be plainer to confine my remarks to research directed to elucidating the works of considerable authors. T. S. Eliot has an interesting passage in his British Academy lecture on Milton in which he defines the provinces of the

academic and the poetic critic. The first, he thinks, is concerned with the past poets' contemporary setting, the second
with the past poets' relevance to modern production. And he
considers that the first type of critic can help the other. This
attempt to link the academic with other types of critic is
much to be welcomed. But surely Eliot makes a large
omission. The value of a dead poet is not only to help
engender more poetry; it is, perhaps primarily, to give
pleasure and instruction to readers who may be neither poets
nor critics. And the chief end of criticism is by informing and
interpreting to help readers to that pleasure and instruction.
And that is the end which all criticism of great writers,
research included, must have in mind if it is to remain
healthy.

Now though the academic critic is competent as no one
else is to put the great writers in their setting in time he must
either recognise his work as incomplete and hand it on to
another man for completion or he must try to complete it
himself by pointing out how his more correct setting of a
writer in his age helps the general reader to a more just
appreciation of that writer. And if he is to qualify as a critic
at all he must have responded sensitively to what that writer
is mainly good for.

And here I want to take issue with those who create an
opposition between the acts of setting a writer in his time and
of appreciating him in this year of grace. Lily Campbell
begins her book on Shakespeare's *Histories* with an attack on
Mark Van Doren for being a purely personal and quite
unhistorical critic. Miss Campbell's is a learned book, which
might well be justified as a contribution to history and which
has its bearing on Shakespeare's History Plays, but she is
not eminent as a critic. Van Doren is a fine, if erratic critic;
and if he pays no attention (and I am not convinced this is so)
to findings like those of Miss Campbell, he risks making his
criticism less good than it might be. My point is that there
should be no *opposition*: the two should not quarrel, but one
should assimilate and complete the work of the other.
Maurice Kelley in *This Great Argument*, a book on the relations of *Paradise Lost* and the *De Doctrina*, did me the honour

of making me represent the impressionistic critics of Milton and attacked me for disregarding the purely historical type of appreciation. For Kelley the setting of a poet in his age, the attempt to see him as his contemporaries did, is the final act of academic criticism and apparently it involves no exercise of the intuition, on which he accuses me of relying exclusively. But if the only way to see a poet is through the eyes of his own age, it is only a handful of scholars who will ever see him at all; and these will see him quite distorted because they will have arrived at their knowledge by other means than the poet's contemporaries did. Further, it was precisely through their intuitions that Milton's contemporaries and immediate followers appreciated his poetry and found him better worth reading than Benlowes or Davenant. Maurice Kelley by writing a book on him at all is simply admitting and following the lead of the intuitions that established that preference. And when it comes to the central critical act, that of appreciation, the intuitions of a modern reader are much closer to the intuitions of a contemporary reader than any scholarly reproduction of contemporary conditions can ever be. But again there should be no quarrel. Maurice Kelley has written a fine book—a work of patient and accurate scholarship—on Milton's *De Doctrina* and *Paradise Lost;* and the critic ought to take it into account when he tries to record what *Paradise Lost* means to him. But, when the critic has taken it into account all he can, it is still no substitute for what the poetry of *Paradise Lost* tells him; just as in criticism generally there is no substitute for the reader's response. That response may be fallible and unsatisfactory, but it is *paramount,* the only ultimate criterion; and to it all factual data, however much they are taken into account, must be subordinate.

I do not mean to say that criticism can deny facts; but the critic's response may have to go against what the antiquarian facts may point to as a greater initial probability. Take a classic example: the interpretation of Hamlet's motives in sparing Claudius at his prayers. The purely historical critics have no difficulty in accepting Hamlet's professed motive for not wanting to kill Claudius except at a moment fatal to his chances in the next world. That motive was perfectly plain and understandable to Shakespeare's contemporaries, and if we put ourselves back in time, as we should, there is an end to all difficulty. The facts appear to support our taking the speech at its face value. Now of course we should take the contemporary opinion into account; but what if, nevertheless, the whole context of the play, the run of the verse, and our impression of Hamlet up to that point persuade us otherwise? Are we *bound* to believe that Shakespeare also accepted that contemporary opinion? It denies no fact to say that Shakespeare might have been more sensitive than the average Elizabethan and might have attributed a greater than average sensibility to Hamlet. The idea that Hamlet had other, unconscious, reasons for sparing Claudius while putting up reasons, untrue for himself but acceptable to the general run of men at that time, is not impossible. And the only way we can hope to decide aright in this matter is, first to know all the facts we can, and then to read and respond, with all the honesty and sensibility of which we are capable, to the total impression the passage makes on us.

And this is my main plea to you if you are literary and not antiquarian researchers. Never forget that the response of your whole self, or of all the parts of it you can muster, to the work of art is the one foundation of criticism—or rather of your own fractional share in the common foundation.

Not that the relation of scholarship to criticism is simple: on the contrary it is a queer affair; and it most reminds me of the mechanism of war. Who has not been struck by a disproportion in modern warfare between the preparations and the execution: between the protractions and grandiosities of all the happenings behind the front and the chances and confusions and shabby agonies of the battle itself? In its grandiosities modern scholarship resembles those preparations. Criticism is like the battle, a chancy and confused and even ridiculous affair in many of its manifestations. And yet it is the only form of action to which the grandiose severities of scholarship can lead and which justifies the kind of scholarship which concerns the works of man's imagination.

Now you may think that my talk has been directed against

research rather than for it. This has not been my intention. I have meant to advocate the practice of the right kind while deploring the wrong. And to end I will give some instances of pieces of writing that have really ministered to that literary appreciation which should be the chief end of research and criticism.

· As you know, a manuscript version of Malory's *Morte Darthur* came to light some years back in the library of Winchester College. From this manuscript Vinaver made a new text and drew certain conclusions. The chief was that *Morte Darthur* was a name not applicable to the whole of the work that passed under it; and that in fact it was not a single, continuous book but a series of disconnected stories, in other words the collected works of Malory. Now this discovery really helps appreciation. We had been judging Malory on false premises and had either to imagine a unity in his work that did not exist, or to accuse him of grossly ill-proportioned construction. We are now in a far better position to appreciate. Vinaver's findings are the more important because (in England at any rate) Malory is the one English author between Chaucer and the Elizabethans tolerably known to the general educated reader. Filtered through the scholars to the general reader they will genuinely promote his appreciation of great literature. W. W. Lawrence wrote a book on Shakespeare's Problem Comedies, the substance of which was to demonstrate that many episodes in the comedies were common in folk lore and much more familiar to the Elizabethans than to ourselves. One example is that of the substitute bride, a motive appearing in *All's Well* and *Measure for Measure*. Now this knowledge is really helpful. Modern readers have been needlessly shocked by a motive, unfamiliar and startling to themselves but conventional to the Elizabethans. By allowing for this familiarity modern readers have a better chance of understanding the plays. In *Kittredge Anniversary Papers* Greenlaw published an article on Sidney's *Arcadia* proving that far from being an affected piece of pastoral escapism it had a serious political theme. This article by correcting a gross error that hampered the appreciation of *Arcadia* for some hundred and fifty years has rendered a most notable service to criticism. Then there are the various editions of the English classics that have either given a pure text or elucidated difficult places. The service these have rendered to criticism is obvious.

These are examples out of a very imposing mass of valuable criticism or aids to criticism carried out in the last fifty years. My plea is not that you should beware of research because of the abuses of it but that you should practise it in the best possible way. It is sometimes said that Canada's mission is to mediate between Britain and the United States. Well, the characteristic virtues of British criticism are sensitiveness and a mature power of reflection; and its vices are amateurishness, snobbery, and deficient energy. (And I am not saying that all British critics have these vices.) The characteristic virtues of United States criticism are energy and curiosity and thoroughness; and its vices are deficient reflection and an issue from facts into more facts instead of into conclusions. (And again I am not saying that all United States critics have these vices.) And my final word is, to those of you who aspire to research: go ahead and combine the virtues of both countries.

Lilies or Dandelions?

I N the 1955 volume of the *Twentieth Century* there was an article by C. S. Lewis called "Lilies that Fester." It includes topics of special interest in Cambridge. I agreed so heartily with some of the things in it that I was tempted at a first reading to swallow blindly certain other things which, on reflection, I think exaggerated or mistaken. Lewis, as a controversialist, commands a rhetoric both delightful and persuasive in itself and rendered all the more so by the conspicuous unpersuasiveness of the rhetoric of much controversy today. For this delight we must be grateful, but Lewis's very success in sustaining it has its dangers; for while it lends truth a fine emphasis it can dazzle the eye of the reader and make him less heedful of the near miss and of the exaggeration.

In his first pages Lewis tells us that by pursuing culture for culture's sake you destroy the object of your pursuit. This cannot be said too often; but surely he goes too far in the degree of spontaneity he demands in the pursuit of those things, poetry for instance, which, sought ultimately for their own sake, lead to that culture of which we should not speak and to which there is no direct entry. He writes (p. 332):

> Those who read poetry to improve their minds will never improve their minds by reading poetry. For the true enjoyments must be spontaneous and compulsive and look to no remoter end. The Muses will submit to no marriage of convenience. The desirable habit of mind, if it is to come at all, must come as a by-product, unsought.

The general doctrine of these sentences is so wholesome that we can easily miss the exaggeration they contain. We all know the real right thing; the boy from the Philistine home staying with his uncle in the untidy house with the big library, pulling one book after another out of the shelves, till a line of Marlowe or a sentence of Macaulay catches his eye and grips his attention and he reads on and on entranced; or, sitting bored in the too familiar dining-room at home on a wet afternoon, he lifts his eye to one of the pictures he has known vaguely all his life and, for the first time, begins really to see it. Of course that is how things *should* happen; but have such happenings been the *rule*, even in less planned and organised ages than our own? Surely, the *purely* spontaneous enjoyment of the arts has always been the exception, while usually some sort of compulsion has entered into the process. In the eighteenth century, apart from the compulsion at school to learn to construe Horace—a compulsion to which C. S. Lewis has no objection—there was a kind of compulsion, if you belonged to a certain section of a certain social class, to give to the poetry of Horace a high degree, if not of appreciation, at least of heed. In the same way, after the first world war, there was a kind of compulsion among readers of good literature to heed and to admire *Moby Dick*. You felt small and mean if you had not done so. Doubtless such compulsion had bad effects on some readers, forcing them to put fashion before enjoyment and to feign a pleasure they never genuinely felt. But more readers either refused to be bullied and if they disliked the book said so, or, having read a few pages, forgot the initial compulsion and continued to read with the same freshness as if they had lighted on the book by accident. In other words, not only is the spontaneous entry into a book exceptional, but a great measure of spontaneity can co-exist with only a small measure of compulsion. Further still, much ultimately spontaneous enjoyment might not have existed at all but for some pressure from without.

Granted that some compulsion is unavoidable, we should try to distinguish the different kinds. Lewis's picture of a "Charientocracy," illustrated from J. W. Saunders's article, "Poetry in the Managerial Age," is ghoulish after the manner of *1984*.

> We get our "co-ordinators" through education; success in examination is the road into the ruling class. All that we need do, therefore, is to make not just poetry, but "the intellectual

discipline which the critical reading of poetry can foster," the backbone of our educational system. In other words, practical criticism or something of the sort, exercised, no doubt, chiefly on modern poets, is to be the indispensable subject, failure in which excludes you from the Managerial Class. And so our poets get their conscript readers. Every boy or girl who is born is presented with the choice: "Read the poets whom we, the *cultured*, approve, and say the sort of thing we say about them, or be a prole."

This is terrifying; and I must admit that Saunders's own words are quite as terrifying as Lewis's summary of the article's conclusions. He looks forward to a reorganisation of education, part of which is as follows:

> At the sixth form and University stage, young people ought to acquire a knowledge of the processes and techniques of critical reading; poetry treated as an intellectual exercise ought to be the staple basis of all curricula, whether in the arts or the sciences, similar to that which Latin and Greek provided until recently.[1]

Nothing could be farther from the truth than this analogy between Saunders's proposals and the old Classical education. In spite of disputes over textual variants and the interpretation of obscure passages there exists an overwhelming agreement about the *sense* of the Greek and Latin Classics which is the modest aim of a large part of a classical education. There is wide agreement that Liddell and Scott, and Lewis and Short, are dealing in certainties. But the "processes and techniques of critical reading"—who is to say what these are with the certainty required for teaching a cross-section of schoolboys, even at sixth form level? Who indeed, unless J. W. Saunders and a panel of his associates? And what hope of imposing their laws except under the most rigid dictatorial régime? And that is where the comfort comes in. However gruesome the conditions Saunders yearns for, their imposition is doubly improbable. First, there is no likelihood that a sufficiently severe dictatorship will be imposed on this country in the foreseeable future; and second, if it were, it would not have the least use for "processes and

[1] *Essays in Criticism*, July 1954, pp. 280-1.

techniques of critical reading" as the backbone of the highest education. In other words, unspeakable though the form of compulsion be that Lewis describes, I find him unnecessarily alarmist in the way he seeks to make our flesh creep; no danger of *that* particular festering of lilies.

Not that things are not bad enough; and with Lewis's remarks on the habit, all too common in schools, of compelling appreciation of poetry I fervently agree. I could not be more horrified than he is at the spectacle of the schoolmaster giving his class poems or passages for study and telling them not only which they must prefer but exactly on what grounds. Indeed, I have had experience, in examining at the University, of the unhappy effects of this procedure. Thus nurtured at school the wretched candidate, having no genuine opinions of his own, makes a desperate guess whether he ought to praise or damn the poem or passage presented to him and, having made up his mind, proceeds to deck the exhibit with the various prefabricated labels of praise or damnation (as the case may be) that have been handed out to him.

To myself, who along with the late M. D. Forbes and I. A. Richards had a lot to do with introducing the criticism of texts into the English syllabus at Cambridge, such an abuse is bitter indeed. We acted thus because we thought that we should be giving able men the chance of saying what they genuinely thought in a way that was not possible in dealing with strict matters of fact, that we were confronting them with the real thing instead of all the marginalia that had come to hedge the real thing round. But that there could be any sort of rigidly right answers was a notion that had never entered our heads. Nor did we suspect that some of the men to whom we had offered the criticism of texts and who had so obviously benefited would carry their enthusiasms into the schools and help to impose there a kind of study only suitable to a select number of men at an advanced stage of the university course.

Which brings me to my last point of dispute with C. S. Lewis. Does he sufficiently distinguish between the two compulsions: the compulsion put on schoolboys of all tastes and attainments to feign a power of judgement beyond their mental means, and the compulsion put on a select number of senior undergraduates to answer a certain kind of question in a subject of their own choosing? If a man chooses to read English, he may be presumed to have some taste for it and thus enters a different category from a cross-section of schoolboys. And the best way of allowing him to reveal his taste is not to ask him generalised factual questions on his subject but to confront him with the particular, with the actual stuff. I readily grant the *Lilies that fester* argument. A set of examiners fanatically certain of having seen the light and of knowing all the right answers could, even at the highest university stage, do far more damage in dealing with the living stuff of literature than in dealing with matters of philology or literary history. But I have yet to encounter such a set of examiners. In reality examiners simply aren't like that. Take this caption of a question recently set in a University examination on practical criticism:

> Kipling's *If—*, printed below, is one of the most read and most abused poems in the English language. Having tried to look on it as if it were new to you, say what you think of it and why. In writing, remember that it was published in *Rewards and Fairies* as a postscript to a story about George Washington and that the examiners in reading your answer do not take sides either for or against the poem.

There is little compulsion left here, beyond the basic compulsion common to all examinations; while a candidate with a direct feeling for literature would be more likely to do himself justice through writing on an actual poem than through answering the question "Describe and account for the widely differing estimates of the merits of Kipling as a poet."

What I fear is that the abuse of practical criticism will create a reaction against it so violent as to abolish its legitimate use. That is why we should take care to discriminate. It would be a pity if, in our anxiety lest the lilies fester, we should dig them all up and play for safety by growing dandelions in their stead.

On Annotating "*Paradise Lost*" IX and X
for Schools

To deal with this topic as I wish means being personal in a way unbefitting a learned journal. But, since for this issue the journal has assumed the more personal guise of a *Festschrift*, it may perhaps allow me the necessary latitude.

Rightly or wrongly, in my work as a scholar I have chosen to write books rather than to annotate texts, except when I anthologised the poems of Wyatt and felt obliged to try to explain such passages in them as seemed to me to need explanation. More recently I wrote introductions to school editions of some of Milton's shorter poems and of the first two books of *Paradise Lost*. And now, concerned with the neglect of the later books of *Paradise Lost* compared with the vogue of the first two, I have been moved to do something about it and have edited Books Nine and Ten for use in schools. This time I could not escape with a bare introduction but had to write the notes also. My experience of annotating proved different from what I had expected and more interesting. It is this experience, with its lessons both critical and educational, that is the subject of this paper.

My first lesson was that more editors had dealt with the earlier than the later books of *Paradise Lost* and that they had concentrated most on the first two. Even so, with Todd's Variorum and the excellent editions of Verity and Merritt Hughes I expected to have little new to contribute myself. I had to allow that Todd and Hughes aimed their remarks at an older set of readers than I was to do; but Verity's edition, both in format and contents was plainly intended for schools. So it was with some surprise, when I began on the first lines of the ninth book, to learn my second lesson: that I should have more work than I had bargained for; that in fact the schoolboy had been allowed an amount of knowledge and a capacity for understanding greater than I should have thought possible, and even that there were things in these books that had been misinterpreted. Milton begins:

> No more of talk where god or angel guest
> With man, as with his friend, familiar used
> To sit indulgent and with him partake
> Rural repast, permitting him the while
> Venial discourse unblamed.

The difficulty here is of course in the first line. And Todd, through Pearce's retort to Bentley, duly records Bentley's noting it. Bentley, recalling that in the poem God when he visited Adam did not partake rural repast, proposed the drastic remedy of emendation. Other annotators seemed to me to quibble in their efforts to justify Milton's text, the most plausible effort being that of Richardson, who tried to account for *god* by the episode in *Genesis* of Abraham being visited by angels. Even so, he has to admit that "God himself, indeed, is not properly a speaker in it" and to proceed to a pretty thin explanation of this absence. Verity has this note:

> *where God;* understand from what follows some word like "conversed", "spoke". The reference is to book viii, where Adam says that the Almighty gave him possession of the Garden of Eden, warned him not to touch the Tree of Knowledge, and then promised him a help-mate in Eve.

But he shirks the difficulty noted by Bentley: that God did not in fact take a meal. This clearly was not playing the game; and having read Verity's note I came to the depressing conclusion that I had taken on more than I had bargained for. On thinking about the passage afresh I decided, desperately, that all the commentators were wrong; that, though *angel guest* referred (among others) to Raphael visiting Paradise, *god* did not refer to Book Eight at all; and that Milton's intention was roughly as follows. When he says *god* he is thinking not of a precise passage in his own epic but of the stories, sacred and pagan, of heavenly beings visiting men in disguise and eating with them. One such is indeed in *Genesis*, as noted by Richardson, and another is the tale, told by Ovid, of Philemon and Baucis, who entertained Jupiter and Mercury disguised as men. In short, Milton says, "I have finished with the type of literature in which heavenly beings pay genial visits to men and eat with them, to which type my account of Raphael visiting Adam and Eve belongs." This seems to me the obvious meaning but it leaves me apprehensive; for how could the commentators have missed it, if it is so obvious? surely there must be a snag? My hope is that annotators of whom I am unaware have had the the same idea. And I hasten to add that I have not often had to accuse the commentators of being flat wrong; my usual criticism has concerned what they have seen good to pass over in silence: a remark which brings me back to the lines of Milton from which I began.

No recent commentator has thought fit to comment on the word *venial* in the passage before us. Experienced in Miltonic usage, knowing his proneness to use words in their basic Latin senses, they have no difficulty in perceiving its connotations. But they are sadly wrong if they think that schoolboys generally share these advantages with them. They might retort that all that needs to be known about *venial* in this passage is to be found in the Oxford Dictionary, but do they really think that schoolboys make habitual use of it? Left alone with our passage, the ordinary schoolboy would apply to it the notion he has of *venial* as currently used. He may have a notion of what a venial sin is and he may think the word *trivial* a pretty close alternative: *venial discourse* might be about the weather or the pruning of the roses in Paradise; a conclusion hardly fair to the actual talk between Raphael and Adam. Or the schoolboy may approximate the sense to *pardonable*, which is very much nearer the truth and yet fails to hit it. There was nothing in the discourse that called for pardon; there was no initial hint of sin, however small: and the word should convey to the reader that the discourse was permitted by God or even favoured by him; see the original sense of the Latin *venia*.

Through the commentators' failure to gloss *venial* I was confronted with the question: what kind of note really matters for the schoolboy? For instance, was it more valuable to point to a rather different meaning attached to a familiar word or to explain the meaning of *impreses, sewers,* and *seneschals,* occurring a little after *venial?* Verity by his acts is seen to think the latter; and I do not deny that the unfamiliar words should be explained: but if I had to say which was the more valuable for the schoolboy's education I should say the former without the least hesitation. Remember that this is a matter not confined to Milton; and here is a parallel from Shakespeare. Which of the following (both from *Troilus and Cressida*) are in the greater need of annotation for the good of the schoolboy's soul? Nestor speaks of the "ruffian Boreas enraging the gentle Thetis"; and it has been pointed out both that Thetis, as a sea-nymph, stands here for the sea, and that Shakespeare may have muddled her up with Tethys, who, as the wife of Ocean himself, has a better right so to stand. Ulysses compared Time to "a fashionable host / That slightly shakes the parting guest by the hand"; and, as far as I know, it has not been pointed out that when Shakespeare wrote *fashionable* he did not mean by it quite what we mean today. Indeed I suspect that most readers of listeners, having the *cliché* "fashionable hostess" vaguely resounding in their ears, make the word mean *smart* and think of the host as serving a *de luxe* hotel or at least a four-star one. Of course in the Shakespearean sense a host could be *fashionable* as well in a humble motel as in the Waldorf-Astoria; and the word means "adaptable to the changes in fashion." My point is that it would profit a schoolboy more to grasp the different sense of a word in a great speech of Shakespeare than to have to remember that Tethys was the wife of Oceanus.

Through such instances we arrive inevitably at the general question of what in fact it profits schoolboys to be put through a detailed study of a few classics of their own tongue. I shall not try to answer this terrifying question; but I shall plead that the education inherent in looking closely at the meanings of words is profitable. It would be foolish to expect that books of *Paradise Lost* or plays of Shakespeare will be read for pleasure in later years by most children made to study them at school. This happy issue will be exceptional. Anyhow, there is no compulsion in later life to read poetry. But no one, not even the man most able to conduct his life-work through mathematical and other symbols, can do without words; and competence in that traffic is one of the first conditions of happiness and success in life. To be aware of words not only enlarges a man's scope but protects him in a world which through the medium of words, seen in print or heard on the air, is, like Shakespeare's Ephesus,

> full of cozenage,
> As, nimble jugglers that deceive the eye,
> Dark-working sorcerers that change the mind,
> Disguised cheaters, prating mountebanks,
> And many such-like liberties of sin.

Train a child to look for differences of meaning in the same word used by Milton and ordinarily by himself and you begin to make him critical of his own use of words and better aware of the power of words as used by others; more likely in later life to ask what the promises and pretentions of politicians and advertisers really amount to.

What I have just said about words began from Milton's use of *venial*. And here are other examples of words which call for similar annotation. When Satan first saw Eve among the flowers he was so charmed that for the time being he was bereft of the power of action and "remained stupidly good." Left to themselves most schoolboys and, I greatly fear, some of their teachers would think that Milton meant by *stupidly* what they mean by it in their ordinary talk. But Milton did not mean that Satan was foolish; he was using the word in one of its Latin senses and meant that Satan was dazed. As far as I know, no recent annotator has pointed this out.[1] More surprising still, when Satan tells Eve that if she eats the apple she will acquire glory by not having been prevented by "the pain of death denounced," the annotators have passed over his words in silence. Any uninstructed schoolboy would take *pain* in its usual sense of *suffering*, would be hopelessly puzzled by the word *denounced*, which in its modern sense will not fit the passage, and could have no idea whether it is *pain* or *death* that is *denounced*. Warned by previous

---

[1] Patrick Hume has a good note, but what schoolboy has access to Hume?

experience he might suspect a Latinism, but only a very gifted and well instructed schoolboy would conclude that Satan's words mean "the proclamation of the penalty of death."

As with altered meaning, so with altered pronunciation. Schoolboys' ears can be trained; and that training will be impaired, if the versification of their texts is murdered by false accents. I still remember one of my class at school reading

'Tis sweet and comméndable in your nature, Hamlet,

and not being pulled up by his teacher. I also remember being vaguely puzzled by the way the line went; but no one ever told me that Elizabethan stresses did not always agree with ours. Todd marks many of the unusual stresses, and Merritt Hughes some. But an annotator for schools should note them all; and as much for the instruction of the teacher as of the pupil. Even at the best staffed universities, with the maximum of individual teaching, it is impossible, through lack of time, to train undergraduates in the reading of verse; and the unhappy spectacle of men getting degrees in English learned in facts and incapable of reading verse aloud in a civilised manner is distressingly frequent. If the teacher is constantly reminded by the notes in the edition he uses of archaic stresses he may be persuaded to take the matter of reading verse more seriously. There are many lines that need thus annotating, for instance: ix, 320, "less áttribúted to her faith sincere"; ix, 511, "At first, as one who sought accéss, but feared"; and probably (cf Italian rimédio) ix, 919, "Submitting to what seemed remédiless." In the same way, if the annotator is at all puzzled by the rhythm of a line, he should say so and offer his tentative suggestion in the hope of arousing discussion. I think that a schoolboy might find the rhythm of x, 423, "far to the inland retired, about the walls" tricky; and I guess that we should read it as, "Far to th'inlánd etc." I believe that such prosodical matters are more interesting and profitable to schoolchildren than the miscellaneous references to Bible or Classics which must indeed be explained for the sake of further profit but whose self-value is minimal.

Alternative meanings are all to the good as providing material for dispute in class and should be pointed out. These lines (x, 28-31), describing Gabriel and his guard making their report to God, give a good example.

> They towards the throne supreme
> Accountable made haste to make appear
> With righteous plea their utmost vigilance,
> And easily approved.

Verity thinks that *accountable* goes with *vigilance*, and the meaning would be: "They, approaching the throne, hastened to make their vigilance, which had been the best they were capable of, appear sufficient for the account they were expected to render; and they vindicated their conduct." But this interpretation, though not impossible, demands the queer understanding of *going* before *towards* and a distortion of the natural word order violent even for Milton. It also demands a rhythm that strikes me as un-Miltonic. I prefer to make *accountable* agree with *they* and to interpret the lines thus: "Knowing that they were to be called to account, they hastened towards the throne in order to make evident that they had watched with the utmost care; and they vindicated their conduct." Todd does not annotate but through his pointing shows that he takes the sense in this way.

If an annotator is defeated by a passage he should own up; and most of all in a book meant for schools. Schoolboys easily imagine that the editors of their texts have some magic access to meaning that costs them no effort. If they can acquire even the dimmest realisation that annotators have to take trouble, to submit to tedium, and can be uncertain of themselves, they will have learnt a useful lesson, which might lead them on to think that some day they may have a right to their own differing opinions. It may even occur to them that the mysterious mortal who annotates from some remote academic citadel could be looked on as co-operator not dictator. I now own up to a passage which has defeated me but which the annotators pass over as if it presented no difficulty. I am much embarrassed, for it is most likely that there is a quite obvious explanation to which I have been blind. This is the passage (x, 332-6):

> He, after Eve seduced, unminded slunk
> Into the wood fast by, and, changing shape
> To observe the sequel, saw his guileful act
> By Eve, though all unweeting, seconded
> Upon her husband.

Why *though*? I should have thought that through unaware-ness Eve was more rather than less likely to play on her husband the trick Satan had played on her. Nor can I find the *though* more apt if it is Adam and not Eve who was unweeting. The best explanation I can offer is lame indeed: that the *though* is retrospective referring to Satan and Eve alone and implying that their two acts were not strictly parallel, for, while Satan knew what he was doing, Eve did not.

There is no harm in school editions being dated through following fashion, for they should not remain in use for long. Thus I did not feel at all apologetic when I yielded to the current proclivity to see double or multiple meanings. I found myself writing notes like these. In ix, 157 Satan, thinking of Gabriel's watch, speaks of ministers tending their earthy charge; and I could not restrain myself from commenting:

> Milton probably wanted *earthy* to mean both *earthly* and *low*. Satan continues to rub in the indignity of angels having to do with their inferior, man. In Milton's day the word could bear both meanings.

And a few lines later when Satan expresses hatred of his animal disguise and contrasts his position of God's chal-lenger to his present case of being "constrained into a beast," I found myself saying:

> *constrained*: another instance of Milton making a word do more than one job of work. Satan says that he is *compressed* into a beast and is *compelled* to invest with flesh and to brutalise his airy and rarefied angelic substance.

Another modern fashion is to welcome rather than to think trivial a play on words. Verity, sparing of critical comments, cannot refrain from expressing his dislike of this passage (x, 92-7):

> Now was the sun in western cadence low
> From noon, and gentle airs due at their hour
> To fan the earth now waked, and usher in
> The evening cool, when he, from wrath more cool,
> Came, the mild judge and intecessor both,
> To sentence man.

Verity was right from his point of view in admitting he disliked the yoking of the coolness of evening with the coolness of God; for he had the opinion of his age behind him, and his readers, sharing his prejudice and ratifying his dislike, would be the more inclined to trust him to do his job of editing well. In the same way I thought it legitimate to say of the passage:

> Milton derived God's visiting Adam and Eve "in the cool of the day" from *Genesis*, but his making the coolness of evening correspond to the Son's "coolness" or freedom from anger is typical of his age. In Milton's day nature existed less as an independent set of phenomena than as a set of human states of mind. The correspondence is much more than what Verity calls "not a very happy play on words."

Lastly, there is the difficult problem of how much aesthetic comment an annotator for schools should allow himself. I am sure he ought not to allow himself much lest he should turn into a dictator whose opinions are *a priori* right and must be memorised and reproduced. On the other hand he ought to give enough critical remarks to show that he minds (for if he does not mind, he has no business to be editing for schools) and to catch the attention of the minority of children possessing a fine intuition for poetry. It does not matter if he is on the wild and provocative side, for the teacher can query his excesses, and children like grown-ups who commit themselves and risk ridicule, provided they are not their immediate relations. Thus I have not hesitated to say things that are likely to be contradicted. For instance, I have detected comic elements in Book Nine, knowing that I am provoking opposition. I have also thought it worthwhile to make a reference or two to wider principles. When we know for certain that Satan is going to find and tempt Eve (ix, 494 ff.), there is a pause in the action and Milton inserts a gorgeous account of the serpent form Satan has assumed. And I allowed myself this note:

> Ornamentation, such as the comparisons that follow, comes best in the pauses of the action. We now know for certain that Satan is to make his culminating attack on Eve and in that certainty we are glad to pause and enjoy the digressive ornament that Milton gives us. The ornament also serves to emphasise what is to follow, hinting that it is too weighty and solemn to be entered on without ceremony. An example of similar technique is in Chaucer's *Knight's Tale*. We know at one point that the rival loves of Palamon and Arcite are to be settled by a tournament and because of that knowledge we welcome the elaborate account of the scenes depicted on the temples of Mars and Venus, where the two rivals go to offer their vows.

The last feeling set up by annotating great poetry is one of bewilderment. What strange stuff it is; and the stranger and the more fascinating, the better you get to know it! And the richer; for if I re-did my annotation I should be amazed at the amount I had missed. What in the world, one asks, can schoolboys make of such richness and complexity? Actually, I think a great deal. But this topic would both take me away from my chosen task and tempt me to intolerable length. I will hold myself and firmly decline its pursuit.

INDEX

Abbot, The, 106
Alastor, 121
All's Well that Ends Well, 21, 202
Allegory in *Merchant of Venice*, 31-7
Allen, Walter, 16
Annus Mirabilis, 155
Anthologies, 185-91
Anti-Romanticism
  English, 130-43
  French, 133-7, 140
  in Cambridge, 140-41
  in Oxford, 137-9
  in USA, 139-40
Apple Cart, The, 115
Aquinas, Thomas, 161
Arcades, 76
Arcadia, 202
Aristotle, 74-5, 159-60
Arnold, Matthew, 134, 157
Art of Donald McGill, 14
Art Poétique (Boileau), 138
As You Like It, 26-8, 66-7
Atkins, J. W. H., 156
Austen, Jane, 125, 132
Author's Apology for Heroic Poetry, 84
Axel's Castle, 142

Babbitt, Irving, 139, 195-6
Bagehot, Walter, 107
Baldwin, William, 166-7, 172, 176-7, 180-81
Bard, The, 92
Barry Lyndon, 15-16
Basis of Shakespearian Comedy, 18, 31
Baudelaire, C. P., 135
Bentley, R., 210
Berners, Lord, 101
Blake, William, 90
Blenerhasset, Thomas, 171-2
Blind Beggar of Alexandria, The, 17, 24

Boadicea, 101
Boileau, N., 80, 83-4, 138
Bowdler, Dr T., 28
Brave New World, 129
Brer Rabbit, 14
Brooke, Rupert, 130, 142
Browne, Sir Thomas, 112
Brunetière, F., 77-8, 83, 136-41
Brunetière's Essays in French Literature, 138
Burke, K., 71
Burton, Robert, 58
Butler, Samuel (author of *Erewhon*), 115
Butler, Samuel (author of *Hudibras*), 125

Caesar and Cleopatra, 125
Campbell, Lily, 165, 199
Campbell, Mrs O. W., 124
Candide, 128
Carlyle, Thomas, 159
Caroline Poets, 173
Cary, Joyce, 142
Castle of Indolence, The, 91-3
Castle of Otranto, The, 100-101
Chaplin, C., 14
Chapman, George, 16, 24
Characters of Dramatic Writers Contemporary with Shakespeare, 56
Chateaubriand, F. A., 134
Christabel, 132
Churchyard, Thomas, 169-70
Civil Wars, 49-50
Clough, A. H., 194
Coghill, N., 18, 31
Coleridge, S. T., 80, 132, 138, 160, 163
Colin Clout's Come Home Again, 58-62, 66-8

Collins, W., 89-98
Comedy and Shakespeare, 13-29
Comedy of Errors, The, 19-21, 23
Comparetti, Domenico, 161
Composition of Shakespeare's Plays, 45
Comus, 76
Condorcet, M. J. A. N., 118-19
Confessions d'un Enfant du Siècle, 135
Conrad, Joseph, 144-53
Contention of York and Lancaster, The, 45
Coriolanus, 69
Courthope, W. J., 137, 157, 169
Craig, Hardin, 49
Critic, The, 101
Criticism
  academic versus appreciative, 199-203
  history of, 154-64
  practical, 207-8
Croce, B., 71
Crotchet Castle, 116-17, 119, 124, 126
Crown of Life, The, 51

Daniel, John, 49-50
Dante, 160
De Doctrina, 199-200
de la Mare, Walter, 142
De Vulgari Eloquio, 160-61
Decorum, 155
Dedication of the Aeneis, 86-7
Defence of Poesie, The (Sidney), 162-3
Defence of Poetry (Shelley), 114, 159
Descartes, R., 83-4
Dionysius the Areopagite, 58
Dolman, John, 165-6
Donne, John, 90, 130-31
Dryden, John, 80-88, 155
  and Classics, 85
  on Lucretius, 81-2
  on Virgil, 86

Earl of Warwick, The, 101
Eastlake, C. L., 102

Egoist, The, 116
Electra, 125
Eliot, John, 186
Eliot, T. S., 141-2, 198-9
Eminent Victorians, 116
Epic Strain in the English Novel, The, 13
Epitaphium Damonis, 76
Erewhon, 115
Esquisse des Progrès de l'Esprit humain, 118
Essay of Dramatic Poesy, 84
Essay on Population, 118
Essays and Studies, 18
Essays of John Dryden, 81
Essays on the Eighteenth Century, 102
Euripides, 125

Faerie Queene, 59
Fair Maid of Perth, The, 106
Faithful Shepherdess, The, 58
Falstaff, 21-4, 44
Family Shakespeare, The, 28
Farce, 13
Ferrers, George, 180-81
Feuillerat, A., 45-6
Flaubert, Henri, 135
Flecker, James Elroy, 130
Fletcher, John, 58
Foakes, R. A., 47
Forbes, M. D., 207
Forster, E. M., 129
Fortunes of Nigel, The, 107
Four Ages of Poetry, 114, 118
Francklin, Thomas, 101
Froissart, Jean, 101
Frye, N., 71

Garrod, H. W., 94, 97
Gascoigne, George, 186
Gautier, Théophile, 135
Glover, Richard, 101
Good Soldier Schweik, The, 14
Gray, Thomas, 92, 96
Grecian Daughter, The, 101
Greenlaw, E., 202

Grierson, Herbert, 130-31
Gryll Grange, 123, 127

Hall's Chronicle, 48-50
Hall, Edward, 48-50
Hamlet, 91, 200-201
Hannay, Patrick, 173
Hazlitt, W., 55
Headlong Hall, 120, 126
Henry IV, 39, 40, 43-4
Henry V, 44, 51
Henry VI, 40-43, 45, 65
  authorship, 45
Henry VIII, 47-54
  Prologue, 53
Heroes and Hero-Worship, 159
Higgins, John, 171, 177-8
History of Criticism, A, 80
History of the Gothic Revival, 102
Holzknecht, Karl, J., 185
Homer, 78, 118
Hooker, Richard, 56-7
Hopkins, Gerard Manley, 90
Horace, 80, 97
Howard, L., 17
Hudibras, 125
Hughes, M., 209, 214
Hugo, Victor, 77, 133-5
Hulme, T. E., 140-41
Humanities, research in, 192-203

Interpretation of Shakespeare, An, 49
Interpretations of Poetry and Religion,
  140
Ivanhoe, 99-101, 103

James, Henry, 142
Jameson, Mrs A. B. M., 30
Jeffrey, Francis, 132-4, 139
Jeffrey's Literary Criticism, 139
Jerusalem (Tasso), 78
Johnson, Samuel, 83, 90, 138-9, 158
Jonson, Ben, 18, 158-9
Joyce, James, 142

Keats, John, 130, 135, 194
Kelley, Maurice, 199-300

Kenilworth, 106
Ker, W. P., 81, 87
Kermode, F., 47
Keynes, Geoffrey, 130
King John, 51
Kipling, Rudyard, 137
Kirschbaum, L., 42
Kitteridge Anniversary Papers, 202
Knight, Wilson, 51-53
Kubla Khan, 132

Laforgue, Jules, 141
Lamartine, A., 77, 135
Lamb, Charles, 55-6, 133
Langhorne, J., 94
Lasserre, Pierre, 137
Law, R. A., 39-40, 43, 45
Lawrence, W. W., 202
Laws of Ecclesiastical Polity, 57
Legend of Montrose, A., 99
Lewis, C. S., 165-6, 204-7
Lewis, M. G., 100
Life in Poetry, Law in Taste, 137
Life of Dryden, 83
Literary kinds and Milton, 13
Literature and the American College,
  195-6
Living with Birds, 17
Lodge, Thomas, 27
Longinus, 80, 160
Lord Hastings, 165
Love's Labour's Lost, 25, 65
Lucas, F. L., 135
Lucretius, 81-2
Lycidas, 76-7, 91
Lyly, John, 102, 125

McClure, E., 185, 187, 189
Machine Stops, The, 192
Maid Marion, 124
Malory, Thomas, 202
Malthus, Henry, 118
Marlowe, Christopher, 56-7
Marvell, Andrew, 112
Maurras, Charles, 140-41

Measure for Measure, 21, 112, 202
Meier, Richard, L., 129
Melincourt, 121-4, 127
Memoirs of Shelley, 120
Merchant of Venice, The, 26
  allegory in, 31-7
  Trial Scene, 30-38
Meredith, George, 116
Merry Wives of Windsor, The, 22-4
Midsummer Night's Dream, A, 24, 26
Milton, J., 74-9, 91, 97, 155, 192-4, 198, 210-13, 216-17
  and epic, 76, 78
  and pastoral, 76-7
Mirror for Magistrates, A, 47, 50, 165-82, 189-91
  dramatic devices in, 176-7
  origins of, 180-82
  political doctrines, 173-5
  popularity of, 171-3
  rhetoric in, 178-9
Misfortunes of Elphin, The, 124, 126-8
Moby Dick, 205
Monastery, The, 99, 102-7
Morte Darthur, 202
Much Ado about Nothing, 26-7, 147-148
Münsterberg, H., 195-6
Murphy, Arthur, 101
Musset, A. de, 77, 135

Nashe, Thomas, 62-3
Nightmare Abbey, 120
Nineteen Eighty-Four, 129

Ode on the Death of Thomson (Ode Occasioned by the Death of Mr Thomson), 89-98
Ode to Evening, 96
Ode to Pyrrha, 97
Ode to the West Wind, 131, 134
Odyssey, The, 178
Of Education, 193-4
Ordeal of Richard Feverel, The, 116
Ortho-epia Gallica, 186

Orwell, George, 14-15
Ozymandias, 108-13

Paradise Lost, 78, 83, 155, 192-3, 199-200
  annotating for schools, 209-18
Paradise Regained, 78
Parrott, T. M.
Pastoral, 58-9, 62, 73-4, 76
Pater, Walter, 157
Peacock, Thomas Love, 114-29, 132
  friendship with Shelley, 119-23
Percy, Bishop T., 101-2
Petrarch, 129, 161
Pettie, George, 186
Picaresque, 14-15
Pierce Penniless, his Supplication to the Devil, 62
Pirate, The, 106-7
Plato, 75, 160
Plautus, 18
Poetics (Aristotle), 74
Pope, Alexander, 160
Pottle, F. A., 102
Potts, L. J., 123
Praz, Mario, 135
Prelude, The, 137
Price, H., 41-2

Racine, Jean, 134
Radcliffe, Mrs Ann, 99-100
Raleigh, Professor Walter, 138, 163
Raleigh, Sir Walter, 57, 59, 69
Reason of Church Government, 75, 78
Redgauntlet, 106
Reeve, Clara, 99-100
Réflexions sur la Violence, 140
Religio Laici, 155
Reliques of antient English Poetry, 101
Research in humanities, 192-203
Revue des deux Mondes, 136
Rhetoric (Aristotle), 74
Richard III, 49
Richards, I. A., 157, 207
Richardson, J., 210

Romantisme Français, 137
Romeo and Juliet, 25-6
Rosalind, 27-8
Rosetti, D. G., 130
Rousseau, Jean-Jacques, 116-18
Rudens, 18

Sackville, Thomas, 176, 189
Sainte-Beuve, C. A., 133-4
Saintsbury, George, 80-81, 87, 156-7, 162, 173
Samson Agonistes, 155
Sanity of True Genius, 133
Santayana, George, 139-40
Saunders, J. W., 205-6
Schlauch, M., 34
Scott, Sir Walter, 99-107
   archaism in language, 100-103
   language of early novels, 99
   language of *The Monastery*, 103-7
Seasons, The, 91, 97
Secretum, 161
Secular Masque, The, 155
Segrais J. R. de, 87-8
Shaaber, M. A., 43
Shakespeare, W., 18-19, 64-70, 91, 102, 147-8, 212-13
   and comedy, 13-29
   and fantasy, 24, 64
   and pastoral, 69
Shakespeare's History Plays, 39
Shakespeare's Problem Comedies, 202
Shaw, George Bernard, 115, 125
Shelley, Percy Bysshe, 108-15, 130-131, 159
   friendship with Peacock, 119-23
Sheretine and Mariana, 173
Sheridan, Richard Brinsley, 101
Sidney, Philip, 55, 161-3, 202
Sitwell, Edith, 81
Six Essays on Johnson, 138
Sixteenth-Century English Poetry, 185-7, 189-90
Sixteenth-Century English Prose, 185-7
Smith, David Nichol, 138-9

Songs and Sonnets, 90
Sorel, Georges, 140
Spenser, Edmund, 31-2, 58-63, 66-7
Southey, Robert, 133
State of Innocence, 83-4
Statius, 85
Sternhold, Thomas, 186
Strachey, Lytton, 115-16
Summer's Last Will and Testament, 62-5
Swift, Jonathan, 125
Sylvae, 81

Taine, H. A., 157
Tamburlaine, 56
Tasso, Torquato, 78
Tempest, The, 70
Thackeray, W. M., 15, 21-2
Thalaba, 133
Thaler, Alwin, 181
This Great Argument, 199-200
Thomson, James, 91-2
Titus Andronicus, 64
To His Coy Mistress, 112
Todd, H. J., 209, 214, 215
Troilus and Cressida, 84, 212
Turgot, A. R. J., 118
Twelfth Night, 26
Two Gentlemen of Verona, 24-5

Unities, 75
Urn Burial, 112

Van Doren, Carl, 123
Van Doren, Mark, 199
Vanity Fair, 15-17, 21
Verity, A. W., 209, 212, 215, 217
Vigny, Alfred de, 77
Vinaver, E., 202
Virgil, 78, 82, 86
Voltaire, 128

Walpole, Horace, 99-102
War and Peace, 16-17
War Song of Dinas Vawr, 114
Warner, Rex, 142

Warren, A., 71
Waverley, 99
Webster, Richard, 171-2
Weekley, Ernest, 102
Wilson, Edmund, 142
Wilson, J. Dover, 43-4
Winter's Tale, The, 67

Wordsworth, 163
Wordsworth, William, 116-18, 163-164

Yeats, W. B., 142

Zuleika Dobson, 17